THE 95TH (THE DERBYSHIRE) REGIMENT IN CENTRAL INDIA

"Lest we forget."

COLONEL J. A. R. RAINES, C.B.,
Commanding 95th Regiment.

[*Frontispiece.*

THE 95TH (THE DERBYSHIRE) REGIMENT IN CENTRAL INDIA

GENERAL SIR JULIUS RAINES, K.C.B.

The Naval & Military Press Ltd

published in association with

**FIREPOWER
The Royal Artillery Museum**
Woolwich

Published by
The Naval & Military Press Ltd
Unit 10 Ridgewood Industrial Park,
Uckfield, East Sussex,
TN22 5QE England
Tel: +44 (0) 1825 749494
Fax: +44 (0) 1825 765701
www.naval-military-press.com

in association with

FIREPOWER
The Royal Artillery Museum, Woolwich
www.firepower.org.uk

The Naval & Military Press

MILITARY HISTORY AT YOUR FINGERTIPS

... a unique and expanding series of reference works

Working in collaboration with the foremost regiments and institutions, as well as acknowledged experts in their field, N&MP have assembled a formidable array of titles including technologically advanced CD-ROMs and facsimile reprints of impossible-to-find rarities.

In reprinting in facsimile from the original, any imperfections are inevitably reproduced and the quality may fall short of modern type and cartographic standards.

INTRODUCTION.

In this 19th-20th century we live at such high pressure, events succeed each other so quickly, political crises and international developments are of such frequent, and often of such startling, occurrence, that not only is it somewhat difficult for us to keep abreast of the times and to preserve some sense of proportion, amid the great incidents, and grave issues, which are almost daily presented for our consideration, but also through want of leisure for reading and reflection we are prone to neglect and forget the history of the past; history which has been made for us by our own immediate ancestors, history luminous with noble deeds and great achievements, and history, finally, which in truth it behoves us to study, and to think on, in order that we may imbibe something of the brave and self-denying spirit which animated those who have preceded us and established our Empire, and that we may strive, as men, to model our conduct, in times of storm and stress, by theirs, and as soldiers, to emulate their gallant acts.

Of all the pages of history in which are inscribed the records of the British Empire, none are more fateful, none more deeply blood-stained, none more glorious, and none more pregnant with solemn warnings and lessons, than those which tell the story of the great Mutiny in India in 1857-58. That was in very truth a time of storm and stress, and even now, after the lapse of more than forty years, as we read of the great upheaval, as we realise the desperate conditions and the terrible odds, as we picture the awful scenes that were enacted, the hardships and anxieties that were bravely and cheerfully endured, the supreme and valiant struggle, and the final victory, we are constrained to say, "There were giants in the land in those days!"

In the spring of 1857, India, generally speaking, was apparently peaceful and quiet. In every cantonment the usual routine was being carried on. The military were busy with their drills and parades; the civilians were attending to their regular duties in cutcherry and camp; the community generally worked and played as was its wont; the shops were open, trade was brisk, and the bazaars hummed with the chatter of gaily-dressed crowds coming and going on their everyday business.

Yet all, had they known it, were walking on a mine. Nor, indeed, were signs and omens wanting to indicate that an explosion was imminent. The Native Army in India at this time numbered about 233,000 men. The English Troops only 45,500; and these were so scattered that mutual support, or any combined action, was difficult, and several important places, Allahabad, for example, were altogether without European garrisons.

But not only did the Native troops at this period largely outnumber the British, but also long years of mis-management and slack administration, coupled with injudicious and dangerous curtailment of the powers of Commanding Officers, had so weakened the bonds of discipline, that the Native regiments at this time constituted in the aggregate a dangerous mob rather than a regular army. At this particular moment—the beginning of 1857—the men, it is true, had no *special* grievance against the authorities, but they were in a suspicious, restless, brooding mood, and it wanted only some small excuse or provocation to make them break out into open mutiny.

This was not long in coming; but first let us note that there were others in India besides the sepoys who were sullen and disaffected. In particular, there were three men who, at this juncture, considered themselves ill-used by the British Government. Each of them represented powerful parties or factions which were ripe for mischief. First there was the King of Delhi, an old man of eighty, who had been informed that on his decease his family must leave Delhi, and that his title would not be revived. The second was the Nana Sahib at Cawnpore, whose memory in connection with the massacres at that place will be for ever infamous. He was the *adopted* son of the Ex-Peshwa, and his grievance was that his demand that his father's pension should be continued to himself had been rejected. The third was the Nawab of Oudh, whose territory had been annexed by Lord Dalhousie in 1856. That this annexation was a step dictated by humanity and necessity alike, has never been disputed, for the iniquitous mis-rule which for a long series of years had made Oudh a theatre for plunder, rapine, and murder, rendered interference by the Paramount Power absolutely necessary. But it is equally true that it gave offence to many, and occasioned a wide spread feeling of resentment and uneasiness, for it was by no means the only annexation made about this period, and it caused others to tremble for their independence.

But amongst the people, too, suspicion and

discontent were rife. Our land settlement operations and the decrees of our Civil Courts had dispossessed thousands of the better class of landowners of their ancient patrimonies; our civilising laws forbidding *sati*, and infanticide, and legalising the re-marriage of Hindu widows, were repugnant to Hindu orthodoxy; and finally, the introduction of railways and telegraphs, the encouragement of missions, and the spread of education, had frightened the priesthood, who, accustomed hitherto to trade on the ignorance and credulity of the people, feared now for their own powers and privileges.

Thus from many and diverse causes the whole continent of India, but Bengal and the North-West Provinces in particular, was in a state of suppressed ferment in the beginning of 1857. The people and the army were both in a highly inflammable condition. It needed but a spark to set the whole mass in a blaze, and the spark was supplied in *the greased cartridge!*

The story of the greased cartridge is an

oft-told tale. It was a new cartridge lubricated with a mixture alleged to be made of cow's fat and lard. The sepoys objected to receive it, on the ground that to bite it (as they had to bite cartridges in those days) would destroy their caste. The enemies of Government industriously spread the report that not only was the cartridge actually contaminating, but also that it was introduced by Government as part of a deliberate design to ruin the men, and convert them forcibly to Christianity. Like wild-fire this story spread from station to station, and from regiment to regiment, with the natural result that it was universally and resolutely determined to have nothing to say to the accursed thing. There were significant outbreaks in connection with it at Barrackpore in January, and again in March, which were suppressed indeed, but failed apparently to awaken those in authority to a real sense of the danger that was brewing. And it was not until the 10th May, at Meerut, that murdering their officers, and all who came in their way, and firing their lines and bungalows, the regiments in that cantonment rose in open mutiny, and escaping to Delhi, raised there the standard of rebellion. The contagion quickly spread, and ere many weeks had elapsed the whole country was in a blaze, with a few remarkable exceptions, due, as in the case of the Punjab, rather to the supreme ability, and energy, and personal influence, of local rulers and leaders of men, like Lawrence, and Edwards, and Nicholson, than to anything else.

Then commenced the great and memorable struggle. Then arose to Heaven the cry for mercy and the prayer for strength. Then was seen what women could suffer, and what men could dare and do. Then, battling bravely against a swarming and a desperate enemy, against a terrible climate, and against disease and death in many hideous shapes, did British arms and British valour after a fierce and exhausting strife, taking a full toll of vengeance for the treachery and bloody deeds of those who had been faithless to their salt, restore at last peace and order to the troubled country. If the cost was terrible, the glory was great, and the lesson learned a solemn and a lasting one.

The story of all these things is fully written in histories and memoirs which abound, and if to many they are a familiar tale, yet they make a record which still heats the blood, and quickens the pulse, as it is told. Who, indeed, can read without a thrill the stirring account of the siege and capture of Delhi, or the dreadful story of Cawnpore, or the narrative of the heroic defence and brilliant relief of Lucknow? Or who can study without admiration the details of the famous campaign of Sir Hugh Rose in Central India, which terminated with the gallant assault of the Fort of Gwalior, and the capture of the notorious Tantia Topi? But to no one can this perusal be of deeper and more abiding interest than to the men of those regiments which bravely bore their share in the dangers and hardships and glories of those perilous times, and amid a thousand dangers, and against overwhelming odds, nobly upheld the traditions of their Corps, and the honour of their Queen and Country.

        H. D. HUTCHINSON, *Colonel*.

SIMLA.

CONTENTS.

CHAPTER I.

	PAGE
Arrival in India — Commencement of the Campaign—Actions of Rowa and Awah, and the Siege of Kotah	1

CHAPTER II.

Capture of Chundaree and Battle of Kotah-ki-Serai . . 24

CHAPTER III.

The Capture of Gwalior 36

CHAPTER IV.

Actions of Powree, Beejapore, and Koondrye—Close of the Campaign 51

APPENDIX A.

Roll and Record of Service of Officers who served in the Campaign with the 95th Regiment — Names of the Sergeants 67

APPENDIX B.

Return of Casualties during the Campaign 83

APPENDIX C.

Itinerary of the march of the 95th Regiment in Rajputana and Central India, from January, 1858, to May, 1859 . 85

THE 95TH (THE DERBYSHIRE) REGIMENT IN CENTRAL INDIA.

CHAPTER I.

ARRIVAL IN INDIA; COMMENCEMENT OF THE CAMPAIGN; ACTIONS OF ROWA AND AWAH, AND THE SIEGE OF KOTAH.

THE 95th Regiment had been at home from the Crimea rather less than a year, when it was ordered to embark for foreign service at the Cape of Good Hope. The Battalion embarked at Kingstown; the left wing, under command of Major J. A. R. Raines, sailed on the 18th June, 1857, in the hired transport "*Polmaise*," while the Headquarters, under Lieutenant-Colonel H. Hume, C.B., embarked on the 26th in the transport "*Beechworth*," Captain Fraine, and sailed the following morning. The Lord-Lieutenant, Lord Carlisle, who had taken great interest in the regiment, and who had presided at a dinner given some months before by the citizens of Dublin to the Crimean soldiers, came down himself to Kingstown to bid the Regiment good-bye.

Just about this time the titles of Grenadier and Light—by which the flank companies of battalions had for years past been known—were abolished, and the companies were then consequently throughout renumbered. This circumstance has greatly increased the difficulty of deciding definitely as to the proper distribution, by companies, of officers and colour-sergeants at this period. However, with the left wing sailed the following officers, viz., Major Raines in command; Captains the Hon. E. S. Plunkett, Foster, Smith, and Stockwell; Lieutenants Benison, Budgen, Waterfall, and Rawlins; Ensigns Fawcett, Holbrook, Macnee, Chapple, Knipe, Wilkinson, and Anderson, with Assistant-Surgeon Fergusson. Lieutenant Benison was adjutant and Lieutenant Rawlins quartermaster of the wing, which consisted of Nos. 2, 3, 4, and 5 companies.

With the Headquarter wing were the Grenadier and Light—henceforward to be known as No. 1 and No. 8 companies—with Nos. 1 and 6, and the following officers: Lieutenant-Colonel Hume, C.B.; Major Vialls; Captains the Hon. E. C. H. Massey, Carmichael, Bazalgette, and Moore; Lieutenants Parkinson, Crealock, Robertson, Bonnor - Maurice, Knatchbull, Bacon, Paske, Fisher, and Willans; Ensigns Pearson, Cubitt and Grote; Lieutenant and Adjutant Sexton, Quarter-master Campbell, Paymaster Morris, Surgeon Ewing, and Assistant-Surgeon Clarke.

With the left wing were the wives of Captain Foster, Lieutenant Waterfall, and Ensign Chapple, while on the "*Beechworth*" voyaged Mrs. Vialls, Mrs. Ewing, Mrs. Sexton, and Mrs. Campbell. The strength of the wings and of the whole regiment was as under:—

Left Wing:

	F.O.	Capts.	Subs.	Staff.	Sgts.	Corpls.	Drs.	Pvts.	Women.	Chldrn
	1	4	11	1	15	13	4	280	18	13
Right Wing:										
	2	4	12	5	25	19	17	353	35	28
Total:	3	8	23	6	40	32	21	633	53	41

The Company Commanders seem to have been as follows: Grenadiers, Captain Carmichael; No. 1, Captain Bazalgette; No. 2, Captain Foster; No. 3, Captain Stockwell; No. 4, Brevet-Major Hon. E. S. Plunkett; No. 5, Captain Smith; No. 6, Captain

ARRIVAL IN INDIA.

Moore, and Light Company, Brevet-Major Hon. E. C. H. Massey.

The Sergeant-Major of the 95th was William Ashfield, who had served throughout the Crimean campaign, and who, after taking part in that in Central India, received a commission on the 1st February, 1867, entered the Bombay Staff Corps, and retired in 1887 with the rank of major. He died in 1892. The Quartermaster-Sergeant was Adam Lambert, who had succeeded in that rank Sergeant-Major Michael McGucken, and who had also served throughout the late campaign in Russia.

The Staff-Sergeants were as follows:—

> Orderly Room Sergeant: William Reid.
> Paymaster-Sergeant: John Hogan.
> Armourer-Sergeant: John Carpenter.
> Hospital-Sergeant: Charles Bramley.
> Drum-Major: Charles McDowell.
> Sergeant Instructor of Musketry: John Bowen.

The Colour-Sergeants were, in the order of companies—Jonas Woolnough, John Brick, James Crangle, John Gooding (who had carried the Regimental Colour at Inkerman), William Turner, George Garrett, Robert Hamilton, and James O'Donnell.

During the week which had elapsed between the sailing of the "*Polmaise*" and of the "*Beechworth*," tidings of the outbreak of the Indian Mutiny had reached England—the last newspaper received on board the "*Beechworth*" containing the telegraphic notice of the outbreak at Meerut—and on the arrival at the Cape of the left wing, Major Raines went on shore for orders; the suspense and excitement on board were intense till his return, when he announced, amidst tremendous cheering, that the "*Polmaise*" was to take in fresh water and supplies, and sail at once for Bombay. Identical orders awaited the "*Beechworth*," which eventually reached Bombay on the 30th October, the clipper-built ship conveying the left wing having reached its destination over a month earlier—on the 27th September. While off Mauritius a fire broke out in the after-hold of the "*Polmaise*," and was not extinguished until it was within a yard of the magazine. All on board behaved with exemplary coolness and courage, and on the report of the occurrence being received at the Horse Guards, the wing was highly complimented by the Commander-in-Chief on the admirable behaviour of all ranks.

During the voyage the left wing lost one man— a sergeant of the name of Fleming.

The left wing of the 95th reached Bombay at a most opportune time, for with the exception of a battery of artillery and a handful of infantry, the city—which was a hotbed of mutiny and sedition— had been denuded of troops. Sailors from the merchant ships in the harbour had been landed, armed, and encamped on the Maidan; the European women and children, who had not already been sent away to the hills, slept nightly for safety on the ships, and it was hourly expected that the native troops in the garrison would rise, murder their officers and all Europeans and Eurasians in the community, and would march off to join the mutineers in Central India, who were flocking to the standard of Tantia Topee. The Chief of the Bombay Police, Mr. Forgett, had ascertained the truth of these statements by venturing, at the risk of his life, to attend a meeting of the mutineers, hidden behind a curtain. The intention of the rebels was to set fire to a large Government store, and while the handful of unarmed troops were engaged in extinguishing the fire, the rebels, at a given signal, were to rush for their arms and commence the destruction of European life and property.

All had been arranged, and the date—the 28th September—fixed; it can, then, readily be imagined with what feelings of relief and with what tremendous enthusiasm did the European inhabitants of Bombay greet the arrival of the "*Polmaise*," *on the 27th September*, with over 300 seasoned soldiers of the 95th Regiment on board.

The wing landed at dawn next morning, every man with eighty rounds of ammunition in his pouches and expecting to have to fight his way on shore. No movement, however, took place; the mutinous sepoys who had been recognised at the secret meeting were at once arrested, and Major Raines was detailed as president of a general court-martial at 11 o'clock on that day, for the immediate trial of three of the ringleaders. One of these was sentenced to transportation for life, but the two others—a drill havildar of the Marine Battalion and a sepoy of the 10th Native Infantry—were sentenced to death by being blown from the muzzles of guns. On the same afternoon of the 13th October at 4.30, the awful sentence was carried out on the general parade ground in presence of the whole garrison, including the regiments to which the condemned belonged and which were themselves believed to be on the very brink of mutiny. The three native regiments were formed up in line of quarter-columns immediately facing—at 200 yards distance—the wing of the 95th in line and a party of armed seamen from the merchant ships in harbour. Exactly opposite each mutinously inclined regiment was a gun, loaded with case, No. 1 of each gun detachment standing by with a lighted port-fire in his hand, and between the 95th and the armed seamen were the two guns to which the prisoners were to be fastened.

The 95th were now ordered to load with ball cartridge, and Lieutenant Budgen, who with Colour-Sergeant Gooding and twenty picked men had escorted the prisoners from the fort, marched his party on to the parade ground. The condemned men seemed confidently to expect a rescue, and their demeanour visibly changed as time went on. The proceedings of the court-martial were then read out and Brigadier

Short directed the mutineers to be lashed to the muzzles of the guns. Colour-Sergeant Gooding now ventured to beg the General not to disgrace the "red jackets" by allowing the men to be executed in them, and he at once agreed and directed their coats to be removed. This was a trying moment; in front of the "thin red line" of the 95th were three strong battalions, while in rear was the native manhood of Bombay City, out-numbering the Europeans present by a thousand to one. On the command to fire the men were blown into hundreds of fragments, the legs and arms remaining attached to the guns and the heads flying back to the rear. The town sweepers were then ordered to collect the remains, and the three native regiments—which had remained perfectly passive during the parade with all their European officers in front of them—were marched away the loaded guns being hand-wheeled after them for a certain distance, but no demonstration was made.

During this execution parade Ensign Wilkinson was on guard and in charge of the fort; he had less than a dozen British soldiers with him, and the native guards in the fort amounted to probably fifty men. "The parade was within sight of the signal mast over a gate which was held by a native guard, whose demeanour clearly showed that they expected a rescue and an outbreak; they had a man in the signal top watching the parade, and they had brought their rifles from their guard-rooms on to the ramparts to be ready to attack the European guard at the mint gate. We had decided to anticipate them with the bayonet if any outbreak took place."

This example—terrible as it was—was most efficacious; all three regiments remained faithful under considerable temptation, while the 10th Native Infantry accompanied the 95th during the whole of the ensuing campaign, and rendered excellent service throughout.

While the left wing was in Bombay, forty men

were sent some two hundred miles down the coast by sea—under Ensign Anderson—to bring in a party of mutineers from Waghotun.

On the 22nd November the left wing embarked on the H.E.I.C. steamer "*Berenice*" for field service in Rajputana, and having landed at Mandavie, in Cutch, the following column, under command of Major Raines, was formed and equipped with transport:

> Left Wing, 95th Regiment, 400 strong.
> Captain Cumberland's Company R. E.
> Six guns, 2nd Field Battery Bombay Artillery.
> Two squadrons Scinde Horse.
> Right Wing, 10th Bombay Native Infantry.

Two days were spent at Mandavie, and on the 26th November the Field Force marched on Boojh, the capital of Cutch, which was reached in three days' time.

The Raja of Boojh was most hospitable and desirous to do all in his power to amuse the soldiers and make pleasant their short stay in his capital. He brought out his elephants and other animals, his jugglers, and his wrestlers. Against these last the men of the 95th were very anxious to pit their own especial champion, and many inducements were held out—for a long time vainly—to Private Lawler to enter the lists. Lawler was rather a small man—a tailor by trade—and when at last he stepped into the ring and saw the huge champion of Boojh, against whom he was expected to do battle, the began to feel that he had entered upon rather a foolish undertaking. However, he circled warily round the native wrestler, and at last—seizing an opportunity—Lawler ran between his legs from behind, and put the giant on his back to the great delight of the attendant "Derbies."

On the 30th November the Field Force marched on Deesa, which was reached on Christmas Day, and where it had been anticipated that the Headquarter wing would join the column. However, the right wing—some 480 strong of all ranks—had not been able to leave Bombay until other British troops had arrived to take its place. On the 28th December the companies had embarked on the steamers "*Berenice*" and "*Lady Canning*" (the Grenadiers in native boats), and reaching Tankaria, in Gujerat, on the 31st, waded knee deep in mud to shore. Thence the march was by way of Baroda,—reached on 5th January—Ahmedabad, and Deesa on Nusseerabad. At Deesa a depôt was formed under command of Lieutenant Waterfall, and here all weakly men, families, sick, and baggage were left. At Ahmedabad, Lieutenant-Colonel Hume fell sick, and left for Bombay *en route* to England, handing over the command of the right wing to Major Vialls; Lieutenant-Colonel Hume, C.B., never rejoined the 95th, but exchanged with Captain and Lieutenant-Colonel Hon. F. Thesiger (now Lord Chelmsford), of the Grenadier Guards.

The Headquarter wing had an uneventful, but wearisome, march to Nusseerabad, escorting a heavy siege train all the way. Brevet-Major Hon. E. C. H. Massey commanded the column, and Captain Carmichael was staff officer, and a heavy job it was getting along the hundreds and hundreds of pack bullocks, each laden with heavy round shot.

On the 28th February, the regiment was again united for the first time since leaving Kingstown the previous June, under the command of Lieutenant-Colonel Raines, who received his promotion as Second-Lieutenant-Colonel on augmentation on the 17th Nov.

In the meantime the wing under Major Raines had met the enemy already more than once since leaving Deesa on the 3rd January; a halt for three days was made at a place called Muddar, whence, on the 6th January, a small force, consisting of four officers and 108 men of the 95th, two guns, and two companies of the 10th Bombay Infantry, proceeded against the entrenched village of Rowa, distant some twelve miles from camp, which was occupied by the rebels and which Major Raines had received orders to destroy. The fortified village of Rowa was built on the side of a hill, the upper part of which was rocky and precipitous. It was defended by a V-shaped ditch eight to nine feet deep, with a mud wall topped with stones by way of a parapet. Its general form was semi-circular, either end resting on and extending up the steep, rocky hillside, but owing probably to the hardness of the ground, and trusting no doubt to the steepness of the hill, the ditch and wall were not so formidable on the extreme flanks, where they blended into the hillside. Major Raines, therefore, decided to attack the place as follows: two companies of the 10th made a long détour, and approached the village on the right flank, on the steep hillside. The country was rather heavily wooded, so this flank movement was not noticed by the enemy; meanwhile the 95th— partly covered by trees and bushes—attacked the village in front. When within about a hundred yards the line lay down, keeping up a steady fire on the parapet, and thus distracting the enemy's attention from the flank movement then in progress. As soon as the flank attack of the 10th was fully developed, and these had fired their first volley, the 95th were ordered to carry the place with the bayonet, which was done with a cheer, the enemy being completely disconcerted by the sudden attack on their left. "During this operation," writes General Sir H. Wilkinson, "we were assisted by a regiment of native auxiliaries armed with bows and arrows, and I believe that their flights of arrows, at their full range, did more execution among the ranks of the defenders than the bullets of the 95th, as the arrows with a high trajectory *searched* the ground immediately behind the parapet, and on storming the place the two first bodies met with were those of men who had been killed by arrows. These auxiliary troops were perfect savages, and later in the day might have been seen returning from the captured village with bunches of men's heads tied together by their hair."

The enemy's loss was considerable; their chief's house was mined and blown up by the Engineers, while the parapet was broken down and the ditch filled in.

Three privates of the 95th—Privates Grady, Hennon, and McQuirt—were severely wounded in this affair, and two men—Privates Bernard McQuirt and William Gell—were specially brought to notice, the former being eventually awarded the Victoria Cross. The first officer over the walls at the assault on Rowa was Captain McGowan, commanding the 10th; he became separated from his men, and being suddenly attacked by three of the rebels, was cut down. As he lay on the ground defending himself as best he could, Private McQuirt rushed in to his assistance. Having shot one of the rebels, McQuirt attacked the others with his bayonet and wounded one, when Sepoy Suddoo Surpuray, of the 10th, came to his assistance and drove off the remaining assailant. In this encounter McQuirt was shot through the arm and received five sword cuts in various parts of his body.

The Sepoy, at Major Raines' special request, was promoted to Naik for his gallant conduct.

An instance of the spirit and pluck of a little drummer of No. 2 Company of the 95th is worth recording. A man in the ranks was severely wounded just as the company was about to storm the village. The youngster helped to relieve the wounded man of his belts—and then slipped them on himself, picked up the rifle, and ran after the storming party!

After the destruction of Rowa Major Raines received orders to march on Awah, there to join a force under command of Colonel Holmes, 12th Bombay Native Infantry, and on the 19th January the two Field Forces joined hands at Jaitpore, a village within two miles of Awah. The combined force now numbered 14 guns, 840 sabres, and 1100 bayonets, and

PLAN OF ROWA

Plan of Entrance

Section

A Point of Assault by 10th N.I.
B "   "   "   95th Regt.
C Position of Skirmishers 10th N.I. in the Hutts
during the demolition of the Houses and Works
by the R. Engineers

[*To face page 10.*

ACTION OF AWAH.

at once marched on Awah, said to be one of the strongest fortified towns in Rajputana, and defended by many cannons and by 2000 fighting men. On passing near the walls the 95th were fired into, when Captain Aitken's Field Battery at once opened fire, and soon compelled the enemy to withdraw within the fort. A reconnaissance was made in the afternoon, the enemy keeping up a smart but harmless fire on all sides, and the camp was then pitched within 1500 yards of the walls. The defences consisted of a mud wall about fifty feet high, loopholed for matchlocks and jingals, and flanked by bastions mounting two and three guns each, the whole protected by a strong abattis. Colonel Holmes, the senior officer, considered the place too formidable to be immediately assaulted, and breaching batteries were accordingly established within from 1000 to 300 yards of the place. On the 23rd January preparations were made for an immediate assault, but that night a terrific storm came on, the darkness was intense, the wind blew a hurricane, rain poured in torrents, and the thunder and lightning overmatched the roar and blaze of our artillery. The camp was truly alive all night, tents heavy with rain, pegs giving way, and the canvas collapsing over the half-drenched and sleepy men. And thus it happened that, in the midst of the tempest, the enemy managed to escape, despite the chain of cavalry and infantry posts, which had been so carefully drawn round the fort that it seemed impossible for the enemy to slip past them. Their flight was first discovered by Brevet-Major the Hon. E. S. Plunkett, 95th Regiment, commanding No. 4 Company, which was concealed in rifle pits within fifty yards of the battlements. When day dawned he thought it strange that no firing came from the fort, and, still stranger, that the heads he saw above the parapet appeared stationary, so he crept out of a pit on hands and knees towards the gate, and still not hearing any noise inside, he soon discovered that the fort was empty.

Considering their weapons, the enemy's defence had been an obstinate one, an incessant but ineffective fire having been kept up upon our camp and approaches from the first, which had led Colonel Holmes to believe that there were at least 2000 men in the fort, but their fire fortunately failed to occasion a single death casualty, although many of the native infantry were wounded. The Thakur of Awah escaped, but about 170 prisoners were captured, twenty-five of whom were shot by sentence of court-martial, they having been taken in arms and in open rebellion against the State. Sixteen guns of various calibre fell into our hands, together with large supplies of ammunition and immense stores of grain.

One man of the 95th came in leading, as prisoner, a huge elephant!

The force remained in or before Awah for four days, employed in destroying and dismantling the works, the palace—a small but magnificent stone building luxuriously furnished—and all the large houses within the fort. The armoury in the fort was full of the most interesting weapons of all kinds, many of which were brought away as trophies by the 95th.

The services of the left wing were acknowledged on the occasion of both these actions of Rowah and Awah by the Government of India, and Major Raines received the thanks of the Governor-General in Council for his handling of the troops at the capture of Rowa.

On the 16th January, Assistant-Surgeon Robert Ferguson, who had served with the 95th Regiment throughout the Crimean Campaign, died at Deesa.

At Nusseerabad a large Field Force was being got together under Major-General Roberts, C.B., for the purpose of marching against Kotah, a large fortified city in Rajputana, about two-thirds of which the mutineers had seized and from which they had expelled the Raja, who, having fortified a portion of the town near the Palace, was there defending himself until succour should arrive. Major-General Roberts arrived

SIEGE OF KOTAH.

before Kotah on the 22nd March, and regular siege operations were carried on until the 30th. The Division or Field Force was composed as under:—

8th Hussars under Col. de Salis.
Two Batteries Royal Artillery under Capt. Aitken.
One Company Sappers under Capt. Cumberland.
72nd Highlanders under Lieut.-Col. Parke.
Wing 83rd Foot under Major Heatly.
95th Foot under Lieut.-Col. Raines.
2nd Bombay Cavalry.
3rd Bombay Cavalry.
Scinde Horse, two squadrons, under Capt. Green.
10th Bombay Infantry.
12th Bombay Infantry.
13th Bombay Infantry.

(The 95th Regiment and 10th Bombay Infantry appear at this time to have, temporarily, formed part of the Second Brigade of the Rajputana Field Force.)

The very day the force arrived before Kotah the enemy fired round shot at the column, but without effect, and that night a party of the 95th, with Carmichael and Knatchbull, went down to the river bank and "broke ground" in two places for batteries, getting fair cover by the morning. This party was relieved about five o'clock in the morning by another party under Ensign Chapple. When these began work in the battery, the enemy brought out two field pieces on the opposite bank of the river and opened fire. Our parties had orders at that time not to fire unless actually attacked; the guns were in the open and without escort and their fire began to get too warm for the working party, so it was decided to give them a few Enfield bullets. Colour-Sergt. Brick and a few good shots opened a fire which resulted in the death of a couple of gunners and the silencing of the guns in a very short period of time.

The fortress of Kotah consisted of a castle built on rising ground on the right bank of the deep and sluggish river Chumbul. The castle, or citadel, was surrounded by a high loop-holed wall, outside which was the town of Kotah. It again was surrounded by powerful fortifications, constructed of cut stone, which completely enclosed the town and citadel except on the river side, which, being protected by the unfordable river, had much lighter walls with numerous small gates. The bastions of the main fortifications occurred at regular intervals all round the town and gave flank protection to the curtains connecting them. They were enormously high, those near the river being from sixty to seventy feet above the water level. Three-fourths of the city itself, including the fortress, was said to be occupied by 7000 insurgents, under one Hira Singh, with ninety to one hundred heavy guns; and these were besieging the remaining fourth of the city, in which was the Palace, and which was held by the troops of the Raja of Kotah. The Raja had never declared against us, but, on the contrary, professed at all times to be a friend of the English and a staunch upholder of the British Raj. The mission of General Roberts' force was to relieve this friendly chief, and to punish the rebels for having burnt and sacked the Residency, and for having murdered Major Burton—the British Resident at Kotah—and his two sons.

On the 26th March about six hundred men under Brigadier Macan—with whom was No. 5 Company of the 95th made up to one hundred strong from No. 6, with four officers under Captain E. D. Smith—crossed the Chumbul River by the ferry near the Raja's part of the town, and took up a position in the Palace as a reinforcement to the Raja's troops. Early on the 29th orders were issued for the assault to take place the following morning; the attacking force was disposed in three columns, the third column—consisting of three hundred men from the 95th, under Major Hon. E. Massey, and three hundred sepoys of the 10th Bombay Infantry under Lieut. Roome—the whole being placed under the command of Lieut.-Col. Raines. As it was anticipated that the enemy would offer a desperate resistance, engineers with explosives were told off to accompany each column, the rear being brought up by two howitzers, while every man was to carry one day's rations and one hundred and twenty rounds of ammunition.

That night Captain Carmichael had proceeded on duty to the left batteries, but was relieved at 10 p.m. by Lieut. Rawlins with a message from Colonel Raines that Captain Carmichael was required to lead the storming party of the 3rd Column consisting of the Grenadiers of the 95th. The operation of crossing the Chumbul river commenced at 1 a.m. on the 30th, the troops being ferried across in boats belonging to the Raja and on rafts made of barrels, each raft holding forty men. The assaulting party of the 95th —Grenadiers, Nos. 2, 3, and Light Companies—paraded at 3 a.m., but as some delay had occurred in the navigation of the flotilla, dawn was breaking before the boats and rafts containing the Derbies emerged from a sheltered landing-place and began to cross the broad deep river, under the eyes of the enemy holding the river-bastions some four hundred yards lower down. They at once brought a gun to bear on the rafts and succeeded in firing three shots before the shelter of the opposite bank was reached. Had the projectiles been canister the rafts would probably never have reached the other side, but being round shot two of them were a few inches too high, while the third was short. The men being all fully accoutred, the sinking of any of the rafts must have had disastrous results.

The plan of attack upon Kotah was as follows: the Artillery to open fire at daybreak with every available gun, whether belonging to the British or to the Raja, and this bombardment to continue until 11 a.m., or until the order for the assault was given. The first and second columns to pass out to the attack from the Raja's part of the town by a forty-foot breach, which was to be made in the wall by our engineers through the explosion of three mines; the third column to move out by the Ketonpore Gate (which was to be blown out), and the Reserve, *viz.*, the troops already in the Palace under Brigadier Macan, to follow. These plans had, however, to be altered, as the engineers found that the wall was so thick that it would take too long to excavate the mine; it was accordingly finally arranged that all the columns should move out by the Ketonpore Gate. About midday the powder bags were placed against the gate, the fuse was lighted, and the sappers doubled back to watch the result.

Directly after, three signal rockets flew into the air, and these were followed by a terrible explosion which shook the ground four hundred yards away; the tremendous violence of this explosion was supposed to be due to the fact that the enemy had undermined the gates, and that when our charge exploded, their mine was fired by it, the result being the entire destruction of the gate and the arch over it. It appears to have so terrified the enemy on the other side, that they fled leaving three guns, heavily loaded with scrap iron, ready primed and trained upon the gateway. When the dust and smoke cleared off, the gate was found to be smashed to pieces; our men poured through in quick succession, but with the utmost steadiness, without noise or confusion, each leader heading his own column on foot. The first column turned to the right, the second went straight on, while the Reserve, under Brigadier Macan, remained halted in quarter column just outside the gate, ready to support in any direction. The third assaulting column, with the Derbies cheering loudly at its head, and Lieutenant-Colonel Raines leading, scrambled over the *débris* of the wrecked gate and turned sharp to the left along a narrow lane, with the high wall of the city on one side and the backs of houses on the other. Down this lane the 95th, followed by their comrades of the 10th Bombay Infantry, doubled in columns of sections, but as they neared the far end, Carmichael of the 95th caught sight of a native with a blazing torch in his hand, stooping by the side of a dark object placed across the road; the man was applying his torch here and there as though trying to set a light to something, but he no sooner realized that the soldiers were close upon him than he dropped the torch and took to his heels. When the Column reached the spot, there lay an infernal machine composed of forty-five gun barrels in three rows, the breeches firmly fixed in teak-baulks, and the nipples so placed in long open troughs filled with loose gunpowder, that if ignited in any spot the whole forty-five barrels—loaded to the muzzle with musket balls, slugs, and bits of iron—would have gone off simultaneously. It was most providential that the trembling hand of the native failed to fire the train, for had it gone off, most of the officers and men in the leading sections of the 95th must inevitably have been killed or wounded.

The whole city of Kotah in front of the assaulting columns was now in our possession. The first column having routed the rebels from their positions, occupied the Soorujpore gate, thus taking the enemy in the rear, for not being aware that the third column was to the left, the enemy fled and crossed the front of this column within four hundred yards, a great number being killed by the Enfields of the 95th. Those who were following, seeing that they would have to run the gauntlet, made for the bastions by the river, and, swinging themselves over the battlements, effected their escape by sliding down ropes, which had probably been fixed there beforehand. Some took refuge in houses and others fled in all directions, while a native officer of the mutineers—pursued by some of the Grenadiers of the 95th—who was riding a grey horse, in a paroxysm of frenzy,

spurred the animal to an embrasure, and, leaping
over, fell fifty feet. Death for both must have been
instantaneous, for when afterwards found stone dead,
at the foot of the bastion, the rider was still in the
saddle.

The bastion where this occurred was one of the
highest; it rested on solid rock and was partly
surrounded by a shallow lake or tank. The ropes
were two in number and appeared to be improvised,
being made up of many bits of different sized rope
and looked dangerously weak for the purpose, and the
result was that when a large number of the enemy
had escaped by this means and had taken refuge on
an island in the lake, the remainder became impatient
and crowded on the ropes so that both of them broke.
Those men who were near the top at the time of the
accident were, of course killed on the spot, but those
near the bottom were only more or less maimed, and
to these the British soldiers let down water in chatties:
of this the unfortunate rebels readily availed themselves, for the spot where they lay was some yards
from the water. But fire was opened on the uninjured
mutineers who were seen to be on the island, and but
few of them escaped. The act of their gallant leader,
who jumped his horse over the parapet rather than be
taken prisoner, showed what splendid soldiers some of
these men were.

After occupying the bastions, the columns proceeded to clear the city, a difficult and dangerous
duty, as many of the houses were known to harbour
desperate men, resolved to sell their lives dearly. In
one high house with a commanding position, the
column under Colonel Parke found eight or ten men,
who had barricaded all the doors, and were prepared
for fighting it out to the bitter end. As it was
impossible to leave this occupied house in rear of the
column, the building was mined and blown up with
its inmates, three men of the 72nd being killed in
assisting the sappers. It was afterwards discovered

SIEGE OF KOTAH.

that Lalla Singh, brother of Hira Singh, the rebel leader, was among the party which perished in this house. In nearly every street was a gun so placed as to sweep its length, while in many instances there were double barricades in front to prevent a rush; here and there, two on either side of the gun, were found infernal machines of fifty barrels each, loaded half way to the muzzle, and duly primed ready to be discharged.

The first column captured sixteen guns, the second eight, and the third column fourteen; in all fifty-seven guns were taken, two-thirds of which were of brass or bronze and of the heaviest calibre; some of the iron guns found mounted in commanding positions, such as the angles of the walls, threw heavier shot than did our 68-pounders. Upwards of 500 prisoners were also taken.

That night the several columns bivouacked in the town, and all looting on the part of the soldiers, British and native, was strictly forbidden, though the Raja's adherents were allowed unchecked to take what they pleased. On the 30th March the mounted troops had been sent across the Chumbul River by a ford some six miles lower down, to take up a position on the right bank of the river to cut off the enemy's retreat in that direction. For some reason, which is not clear, no pursuit was attempted for over two days after the capture of Kotah; by this time the rebels had secured so long a start that not only were they not overtaken, but they got away with treasure estimated at six crores of rupees, and much loot from the city. It was reported that 4000 of the rebels with 900 mounted men and ten field guns had fled to an impregnable hill fort called Salumbah, about eight marches distant, and they were never followed up. Major Hon. Eyre H. Massey, who had commanded the 95th reserves in the attack on Kotah, was appointed Commandant of the town, the Raja of which had to pay twenty-five lakhs of rupees to " John Company for the redemption of his city and for his own restoration to the throne.

It was at Kotah that the 95th captured the Ram, which accompanied the Regiment during the rest of the campaign in Central India. As the 95th was moving through the city, a fine fighting ram with immense curved horns was noticed tethered by a temple. The Colonel's attention being called to the animal, he directed Private Sullivan of the Grenadier Company to take him prisoner. The Ram followed Sullivan quite contentedly, and marched 3000 miles at the head of the Regiment through Central India, was present in six actions, and received equally with the rest of the battalion on parade at Poona in 1862, the Indian Mutiny medal with clasp for "Central India."

He was accidentally drowned in 1863 by falling into a well in Hyderabad, Scinde.

In the attack on the city, the 95th had only lost two men—Privates Green and O'Neill—killed, but a terrible explosion on the 31st deprived them of a gallant officer.

The night before the assault on Kotah, the Captain of No. 1 Company, Evelyn Bazalgette, had told Colonel Raines that he felt sure of being killed, and begged him to see that his sword and certain other things were sent to his relatives.

The Colonel laughed and said "presentiments" were all nonsense, but Captain Bazalgette shook his head and said he felt certain that he was doomed. After the city had been taken and the fighting was over and the 95th was marching to camp, Colonel Raines came up to Bazalgette and said, "Well, Bazalgette, I'm glad to see you safe and sound; your presentiment has come to nothing after all."

"No," replied Bazalgette, "but I had a narrow escape, for my right hand man was badly hit."

That night the third column was ordered to encamp about two miles down the river on the right bank, but hardly were the tents pitched before the 95th and

10th N. I. were each ordered to detail a Company for picquet duty to the east to occupy the vacated rebel entrenchment and a village. The next Company for picquet was No. 1, Captain Bazalgette's. The Company fell in and moved off to its ground, passing on its way the destroyed Residency, where there were still blood-marks on the floor and walls, showing but too plainly signs of the brutal murder of the Resident and his family.

Bazalgette, with whom was Lieutenant Parkinson, found that the village was full of combustibles, the enemy having evidently used it as a sort of magazine, loose powder lying about in open *chatties*. Captain Bazalgette sent word to the Brigadier (Macan) who sent down the Brigade Major, Captain Bainbrigge, to see what arrangements could be made regarding the explosives. The two entered the village together, when a native was seen to rush out of a long, low wooden shed, near to which they were standing, and a few moments after came a blinding flash of fire and a dull roar which made the earth heave and tremble. When the dust and smoke had cleared away, it was found that the shed had disappeared, while the bodies of the two officers had been literally blown into shattered pieces of humanity and were quite unrecognisable. Captain Bazalgette's *hand* was identified, both by the ring which was found on his finger, and by the traces of the wound received at the Alma when carrying the Colours of the 95th.

As the explosion took place, many natives ran out from the outlying portions of the village; several of these were sabred by Lieutenant Jenkins, who had at one time been in the "Blues," and was at this time attached in some capacity to the 8th Hussars, and who happened to be riding near the village at the time. The man who had fired the magazine did not escape, being killed by Lieutenant Parkinson of the 95th, when making off with the burning fuse in his hand. Lieutenant Parkinson also secured some fifty prisoners (mutinous sepoys) barricaded in the neighbouring houses, and brought them into camp. A sentry of the 10th Bombay Infantry—Sepoy Shaik Kaddum—behaved at the time with exemplary coolness and courage: he was on guard over some tumbrils near the magazine, portions of which continued to explode for nearly ten minutes; although several of his guard were killed and the nature of the stores in his charge greatly increased his danger, he never left his post, but was found by Captain Ballard, A.Q.-M.G. (who galloped up on hearing the explosion), marching steadily up and down on his beat, though covered with dust and rubbish and bruised by falling stones.

The remains of the two unfortunate officers were placed in one coffin (there being no possibility of getting more than one made in the time available) and were buried by torch-light that night in a grove of palms, Captain Carmichael, who had succeeded Bainbrigge as Brigade Major, reading the burial service. The funeral was attended by the whole of the 95th Regiment and the 10th Native Infantry, by all the officers of the Brigade, and by detachments from every corps in camp. The regimental Colour of the 95th, still stained with his blood when wounded under it at the Alma, was used as a pall to cover the coffin containing poor Bazalgette's remains.

For a week or ten days after the fall of Kotah, the force was encamped outside the town, but soon after this it was broken up, the 83rd Regiment and the Batteries, with the 12th and 13th Bombay Native Infantry returning to Nusseerabad, while the 72nd Foot marched to Neemuch. A flying brigade was then formed to co-operate in Central India with a column under Major General Sir Hugh Rose, K.C.B.; this brigade was placed under the command of Brigadier Smith, 3rd Dragoon Guards, and was at first known as the Rajputana Field Brigade; it was made up of the 8th Hussars, the 95th, the 3rd troop

SIEGE OF KOTAH.

of the Bombay Horse Artillery, two squadrons of the 1st Bombay Lancers, and the 10th Bombay Infantry.

The following divisional order was issued by Major-General Roberts on the fall of Kotah:—"The Major-General Commanding cordially congratulates the forces under his command on the successful result of yesterday's operations, and offers his best thanks to officers and men for the zeal and steadiness with which the necessarily hard duties have been performed, preparatory to the assault which crowned their labours yesterday."

Captain Carmichael, having been appointed Brigade-Major to Brigadier Macan's brigade, was here separated for a time from the 95th Regiment, and did not rejoin until the 5th November (Inkerman Day), when he crossed from Neemuch to Deepnakhaira with a small escort of Sikh Horse, and accompanied by a Lieutenant Barnes—then on his way to join a regiment of native cavalry—who many years later filled the post of Herald at the Delhi Imperial Assemblage.

CHAPTER II.

CAPTURE OF CHUNDAREE AND BATTLE OF KOTAH-KI-SERAI.

TOWARDS the end of April—on the 23rd—Brigadier Smith's column left Kotah under secret orders: it was at first supposed that its destination was the rock-fortress of Salumbah, whither the Kotah rebels had betaken themselves, and the Brigade started in high spirits at the thought of the prize money awaiting them. Nothing leaked out until the column had been ten or twelve days on the march, when it transpired that the strong fort of Chundaree was its destination. Chundaree had been captured on the 10th March by a field force under Sir Hugh Rose, but on his leaving the neighbourhood the rebels—chiefly Bundeelas—returned in strength, drove out the hundred men of the 25th Native Infantry who were holding it, and again took possession of the fort.

On the 7th May one Company of the 95th was detached with the 10th Bombay Native Infantry, and this little force attacked and destroyed Man Sing's stronghold of Padoon: twenty prisoners were taken and were disposed of by drumhead court-martial.

Goona, on the Grand Trunk Road, was reached on the 12th May, and on the 24th (the Queen's Birthday) the Force—now known as the 3rd Brigade Central India Field Force—arrived within a march of Chundaree. On the following day the Column marched to a place called Koondwarra, within three miles of the fort, and a reconnaissance was sent out under Captain Fenwick, Field Engineer, and reached the old palace at Futtehabad, where it was fired upon. The

CAPTURE OF CHUNDAREE.

party, however, seized a strong line of masonry defences which extended across the valley, and the enemy retreated in haste to the fort. The Brigade then marched to its encamping ground, and another reconnoitring party of a hundred men of the 95th was sent out to the eastward in the afternoon, and took possession of the village of Ramnugger. Leaving fifty men to occupy a stone house, the camp was pitched in the plain to the west of the village, while a party of the 95th and 10th Bombay Infantry, supported by four guns and a squadron of the 8th Hussars, advanced up the valley in skirmishing order and took possession of a picquet house at the head of the valley, driving out the enemy, who retired firing. As soon as it was dark, the artillery brought up two 8-inch mortars and planted them on a ridge to the left of a tunnel, by the picquet house, and within 1,400 yards of the fort walls. Throughout the night working parties were employed in throwing up a breastwork, and a lodgment was effected within four hundred yards of the right bastion, by a party of Sappers supported by forty men of the 95th, and loopholes were made in an old wall as an advanced picquet post.

On the evening of the 25th May, the camp was visited by a terrific storm; every officer's tent but one and those of nearly all the men, together with the officers' mess tent, were blown down and everything was drenched with the rain, which fell in torrents. In consequence of the state of the tents, the force was unable to march on Chundaree till 3 p.m. on the 26th; this march—although a short one—was about the hottest and most trying of the whole campaign, upwards of thirty cases of sunstroke occurring. Colonel Knatchbull, who relates the above, characteristically adds, "It was Derby Day—Beadsman's Derby!"

By noon the next day brushwood was collected and gabions made to fill up the deep ditch—cut out of the solid rock—to enable the assaulting party to cross over to the breach made in the bastion by the guns. The troops were in high spirits expecting to have a good hand-to-hand fight, the 8th Hussars, under Colonel de Salis, being concealed by the thick jungle ready to cut off the retreat of the rebels; but at daylight, on the 28th, when the guns were about to open fire, it was found that the fort had been successfully evacuated, and there was nothing to do but to march in and re-occupy it. As supplies were running short, only four days were spent at Chundaree, after which the Brigade returned to Goona and there rested for ten days. The heat by this time was already very great in Central India, and two men of the 95th —Privates Ashbrook and McGarry—had died on the march to Chundaree from the effects of the sun.

On leaving Goona the Brigade started northwards on a dull uninteresting march towards Seepree: dull it was, because at that time there was no apparent prospect of any more fighting, and the retention of the Brigade at Seepree was simply a strategic movement, in order that the Force might act as a reserve and be near at hand in case its services should be required by Sir Hugh Rose, who was then concentrating his forces to attack Jhansi and Kalpi. Brigadier Smith's Column was therefore ordered to Seepree—seventy miles south of Gwalior and forty west of Jhansi—to watch the rebel Jai Dyal, who had escaped with his followers from Gwalior. Marching in the hottest part of the year, the Brigade reached Seepree on the 6th June without seeing an enemy, and found a ruined and deserted town, which had a month before been burnt and looted by the mutineers marching to Jhansi to assist the Rani.

At the end of April there seemed reason to believe that little more remained to be done in Central India by such a force as Brigadier Smith's—except, perhaps, to annihilate the fugitives who had escaped from Sir Hugh Rose, and to deal with the scattered remnants

CAPTURE OF CHUNDAREE. 27

of Jai Dyal's gang. This impression was confirmed by the complete discomfiture of the notorious rebel Tantia Topee and of the Nawab of Banda in May at Kalpi. In the meantime, however, the Gwalior mutiny had broken out, and the Maharaja Scindiah's trained troops, both infantry and artillery (including the battery of six brass guns presented to him by the Government), had gone over in a body to Tantia Topee, the beaten rebel from Kalpi, who was now marching on Gwalior; and Sir Hugh Rose, after bringing together divisions from Jhansi and Kalpi, was about to pursue and finally disperse the menacing band of mutineers. So, countermanding the march of the Hyderabad Contingent, Sir Hugh Rose sent orders to Seepree for the direct advance on Gwalior—distant seven marches—of Brigadier Smith's force. The march —at this hot time of the year—was performed with wonderful rapidity, the Brigade reaching Kotah-ki-Serai on the 17th of June, almost at the very time that Sir Hugh himself, advancing from the opposite direction, was fighting his way into Morar Cantonments, four miles from and to the east of Gwalior. Smith's Brigade had marched ten miles from its camping ground of the 16th June, and had reached Kotah-ki-Serai at seven in the morning; the 95th were just beginning to pitch tents and to prepare breakfast, when the whole force was startled to hear a gun fired from the heights to the north and to see a round shot bounding into the camp. This was the opening of the ball, for at once the bugles sounded the "assembly," and soon after the infantry of the Brigade, commanded by Lieut.-Colonel Raines was formed up.

"The column was halted, and the Brigadier started off with his staff to reconnoitre; the troop of the 8th Hussars from the advance guard accompanied him as an escort, likewise two or three officers of the company

By the late Major-General J. N. Crealock, C.B., in *I'm Ninety-five* for January, 1885.

of the 95th in some unexplained capacity; the staff officers went off in different directions, while the General rode towards the nearest hill. The ground all round was broken by ravines, and communication became difficult, when suddenly we rode into what seemed a semi-circle of musketry. It was a surprise and no mistake; the words "fours about" were distinctly given by some one *not* in command of the escort, and promptly obeyed—luckily the smoke of the volleys and the dust caused by the wheeling troop hung heavily in the morning air, for all the party had not succeeded in obeying the order. The Brigadier was down on the ground with his horse killed, the two infantry officers and the trumpeter—Barter by name—were close to him at the time, and unluckily no one else saw the occurrence. The Brigadier was, however, only stunned and regained his manners before his recollection of events, insomuch that he refused to accept a mount offered by one officer, and resolutely argued that it would be injudicious to retire until he had found his pistol. As he was a General and the other officers young and inexperienced, a search was set on foot, and the pistol was found; he was then induced to mount the trumpeter's horse. It is needless to say that Trumpeter Barter—holding on to a stirrup—had to go at a rapid pace, as the little party briskly beat a retreat without further controversy, followed by a few shots. The escort would appear not to have realised the mishap, and it was only on the Brigadier's return to the column that the question "where's the Brigadier" received a satisfactory answer."

"The Brigade had meantime been drawn up, I think, in line of columns, and a change of front about half-right must then have been ordered. (The 95th—five hundred bearded sunburnt men, in once-white sea-kit smocks and tattered blue trousers—here and there bare feet, here and there native slippers—while for head-dress the Kilmarnock forage cap with a white cover did duty, sometimes assisted by a towel or a roll of coloured cotton). No. 1 Company, whose fortunes I am narrating, was now on the left in échelon: its commander, on rejoining it, found no orders had been given, so he covered the left flank of the advance which was now ordered, since it was manifestly impossible to pitch camp where we were with an enemy in position on the neighbouring hills. The direction of the advance of the company soon brought it to the scene of the ambuscade, and the reason why the enemy had not followed up their fire became evident, for a deep and broad water-dyke, concealed by bushes, separated them from us—moreover, the dust and smoke and this cover had screened the Brigadier's mishap for a time. No. 1 Company was the old Grenadier Company, and still retained in its ranks the tallest men in the Regiment, and they made but small work of the dyke; but their commander, unlike them, had not been selected on account of his stature, or indeed on any grounds but his seniority as a subaltern, so he would have miserably perished had not his stalwart subaltern assisted him. The men were too eager to try conclusions with the rebels we saw retiring before us, and required forcible Saxon to recall to them the fact that the fortress of Gwalior could not and ought not to be captured by them alone. We found a comfortable spur to extend on, and from this we kept up a disagreeable fire on the enemy's cavalry, who tried to approach us. Meanwhile we heard firing from the line on our right, now separated from us by some four or five hundred yards; the sun meantime was well over us, and the exertion of the night march and morning's scouting began to tell on the men, who were faint too from want of food. A wing of the Battalion had been in reserve, and as they now relieved our wing, we were ordered to retire to our right rear. We then found that we had more men down with the sun and exhaustion than we could carry back, so we retired to a neighbouring knoll from which we could cover the ground; the poor fellows were stretched about, exposed to the fierce sun,* while the enemy's cavalry hovered round us, but our Enfields soon drove them off. We could see on the hills above us a vast concourse of the rebels, many of them in red, while new batteries were constantly opening fire. We were told that they had that day sixty-two guns on the hills; it was also stated that about this time the Rani of Jhansi was killed by a rifle bullet—(some say by a carbine bullet fired by one of the 8th Hussars)†—by all accounts she must have been a brave woman; she was mounted on horseback when killed and dressed in man's clothes. Soon after some of the 8th Hussars relieved us of anxiety about our scattered sun-struck men, and we were recalled to the main body, whom we found with arms piled trying to breakfast off water and native tobacco."

"The enemy had been found in great force, and it was considered advisable to do no more than throw out some companies in advance, while the baggage animals were closed up; we lay down by our piled arms in the noonday sun, but we had found the enemy again, after marching for two and a-half months and seeing none, so we had something to talk about, and the bheesties found us water, so we might have been worse off. About noon, so far as I can recall, we heard a rumour that the baggage was attacked, so the 8th Hussars and the Bombay Lancers had to move to the rear to see to it. The time passed very slowly with us, and many a man lay sleeping in the sun only to awake with sunstroke. I cannot recall any food passing our lips up till then. A subaltern was

---

* Five officers and eighty-four privates of the 95th were this day struck down by the sun. One private—J. T. Watson—died. In June thirteen, and in May eight men of the 95th Regiments died from the effects of sunstroke alone.

† Lance-Corporal Timothy Abbott, of the 95th, also claimed to have fired the shot which killed the Rani.

not in the way of knowing the councils of the Chiefs, so it became monotonous, and it was with a feeling of relief that we saw our ever-watchful and energetic junior Major, Massey (afterwards Lord Clarina), galloping towards us from a neighbouring hill to say a company was cut off by the enemy. I cannot recall hearing any orders, but no doubt they were given, for the four companies instantly fell in, formed fours and hurried off in the direction pointed out; we even went so far as to "double," but Colonel Raines judiciously checked our ardour, for, indeed, we were not in doubling plight. No. 1 Company led, and as its leading section of fours topped the rise, a mass of the enemy several thousands strong, was seen hurrying past below and across our front at about three hundred yards distance; but, alas! our drill-book then (and now) did not help us to do more than—"right wheel, halt, front." When we had reached a point where the right of the line was to rest, a waste of valuable minutes ensued while we had thus to drill, but the spatter of musketry soon warmed into a continuous roll and the enemy soon became hidden from our view; meantime, the Company, under command of Lieutenant Bonnor Maurice, whose safety had been imperilled, had caught sight of the flashing bayonets as we hurried up; he was then retreating at right angles to our line of advance, and this body of the enemy—ignorant of our movements—getting between us, he at once sounded the "advance" and turned on the rebels at the same moment as we came on them."

"A squadron of the 8th Hussars under Captain Heneage, with Captain Poore, commanding the 2nd troop, had followed us, supported by one or two squadrons of the 1st Bombay Lancers; these, as our fire slackened, advanced over the low ground round our left flank, and passed from our view into the dust and smoke below. We helped them with a cheer, and—so some of them said—a volley over their heads, but this I deem to have been a fancy caused by an Indian sun upon an empty stomach! A clash of steel below us, and beyond the dust and smoke issued flying figures, followed by a compact body of horsemen still riding knee to knee. The Horse Artillery thundered after them, and a general advance took place."

General Sir Henry Wilkinson writes: "The general advance at the battle of Kotah-ki-Serai was made at about noon, and the force soon found itself advancing through a fairly open gorge in the semi-circular belt of hills which partly surround the town and parade ground of Gwalior. The enemy retired slowly, but continued to harass the column from the heights on our left hand. Captain Stockwell twice asked leave to take his company up these hills and drive back the enemy, and it was not till the third application—when the fire of the enemy was becoming serious—that he accepted as consent the silence of his C.O., and dashed at the hill with his own company and part of No. 2. The enemy continued to fire until we were within a few feet of them, when they retired and were followed up over the undulating crests of these hills for probably two miles until the further margin was reached, whence we looked down on the Plain of Gwalior. The parade ground was literally covered with troops of all arms, artillery, cavalry and infantry, some of the mutineers still wearing their red coats. We were nearly two miles from any support, but Stockwell's audacity was unbounded. We found an abandoned gun which he insisted on turning against the enemy, and fired a long shot into the middle of them! This resulted in a body of cavalry being detached to attack us, and we had to commence a retreat. It was now long past noon of one of the hottest days of an Indian summer, and the men began to faint from heat, exhaustion, and thirst. The officers relieved them of their rifles, and by giving them an arm helped them along; Stockwell at one time was carrying four or five rifles. I—who was fond of shooting and supposed to be a good shot—was told off as a sort of rear-guard by Captain Stockwell, and two or three men with clean rifles supplied me with them ready loaded, and whenever the enemy came dangerously near I opened fire upon them. This, after two or three trials, kept the enemy from making any direct attack upon us, but the sun was by far the more dangerous enemy, and the heat was frightful. We had had little to eat or drink since marching at two o'clock that morning, and the agony of thirst was beyond all description. At last we reached a muddy pond through which the Artillery had recently galloped and in which there was at least one killed horse. The water was like pea-soup, but we all drank of it, and this was the cause of much subsequent sickness. Major Plunkett and Dr. Clark were two of the officers who accompanied this party."

To resume General Crealock's story:—" Seated on an eminence by himself, the writer disconsolately watched the movement, for an accident of a temporary nature* made walking painful; but luck brought Major Massey on the scene again, and with a spare pony, he was enabled shortly to rejoin the battalion. It must have been then about four p.m.; the infantry were lying down, and the cavalry preparing to dismount after their return from riding through the enemy's camp and capturing several guns; but from our front, from the left rear, and from the right front came round shots lobbing along, and it was evident that we had not yet found a resting place for the night; against this converging fire our Horse Artillery popguns were useless. It was now a question what to do; casualties from the sun and enemy were many; the sun was getting low, our baggage and sick were far away, and our position utterly untenable.

"'Let the 95th drag back the guns captured by the cavalry before they retire,' shouts a hearty old

---

* Major-General Crealock had been wounded.

Bombay Colonel, who had lately joined us, and who looked as if he had not missed a meal since he first eat John Company's salt. 'The 95th will have as much as they can do to drag themselves back,' was the unsympathising answer of Colonel Raines, and he was about right. That retreat was not an hour of pleasure; the bheesties had no more water, the men were quite exhausted, and many could not carry their rifles; but the cavalry officers helped us, and the limbers and carriages of the guns were loaded with men; as a sun-struck subaltern of No. 1 Company required the pony the writer had annexed, he had to content himself with a bheestie's bullock, and thus with a bundle of a dozen Enfields on the empty water-bag in his front, the Commander of No. 1 dejectedly followed his Company, which was now the rear-guard. That night, about eight, we got some food. It is twenty-six years ago, but the impression is vivid on the writer's mind that, had the enemy hardened their hearts that night and attacked us, very few could have stood to their arms. Twenty-six hours without food, a seventeen-mile march, and a twelve hours' engagement with an enemy under a June sun take the 'go' out of the best of us."

The casualties that day in the 95th Regiment were—

Lieutenant J. N. Crealock (wounded).
Private W. Hall (dangerously wounded, since dead.)
Private R. Dutton (severely wounded in the hip when his company advanced to assist Lieutenant Maurice's Company).
Private J. Suttle (severely wounded).
Private J. Bird (severely wounded).
Private J. Swan (slightly wounded).

Sir Hugh Rose in his despatches wrote as follows:—
"They had to contend not only against the rebel army fighting as usual with all the advantages on their side of very superior numbers and knowledge of the

BATTLE OF KOTAH-KI-SERAI.

ground, but they had to encounter also a new antagonist—a Bengal sun at its *maximum heat;* this formidable ally of the rebels' cause was more dangerous than the rebels themselves; its summer blaze made havoc amongst troops, especially Europeans, who, already exhausted by months of over-fatigue and want of sleep, by continued night watchings and night marches, were often exposed to its rays, manœuvring or fighting from sunrise to sunset. The thermometer was at 118° before Kalpi, and on the march to Gwalior it *burst* in an officer's tent at 130°!"

Brigadier Smith in his report on the operations of the 17th said:—" I have only to add that I cannot speak too highly of the steady and soldierlike conduct of both officers and men of the 95th Regiment and of the 10th Native Infantry, who, though exhausted by fatigue and want of food, stormed the heights under a burning sun and a heavy fire."

The following officers and men were mentioned in Sir Hugh Rose's despatches on the battle of Kotah-ki-Serai, viz.: —

- Lieut.-Colonel Raines, commanding H.M.'s 95th Regiment (special mention), good service in assisting to take and hold the position of Kotah-ki-Serai.
- Major Vialls, Major Massey, and Lieutenant and Adjutant Sexton, H.M.'s 95th Regiment, good service on the same occasion.
- Captain Foster, H.M.'s 95th Regiment (special mention), good service in supporting with gallantry and ability the charge of the 8th Hussars.
- Lieutenant Maurice, H.M.'s 95th Regiment (special mention), good service on the same occasion.
- Privates Murphy and Loix, H.M.'s 95th Regiment, gallantly and ably serving captured guns.

CHAPTER III.

THE CAPTURE OF GWALIOR.

On the 18th June, the day after the battle of Kotah-ki-Serai, a junction was effected between Smith's Brigade and the Central India Field Force from Morar under Sir Hugh Rose. This force had fought an action on the 16th, defeating the rebels and driving them with loss from the cantonments, which were occupied. The 18th was devoted by Sir Hugh Rose to reconnoitring the various positions held by the Rao Sahib and the Nawab of Banda; these had with them twelve or fifteen thousand mutineers, chiefly rebellious sepoys from the Bengal Army. The casualties in the 95th Regiment this day were two privates wounded.

"At the first break of day on the 18th, No. 1 Company was paraded and marched off to relieve the most advanced outpost towards Gwalior; we were all pretty stiff with the previous day's work, and not much rested by a hard bed. The dawn of day has always a beauty of its own, except perhaps on a parade ground, and as we sat on the rocky eminence of our post gazing on the gloom which lay below the fortress, I fancy many a one felt the charm of the scene and perhaps wondered if he would see the sun set that day.

By the late Major-General J. N. Crealock, C.B., in *I'm Ninety-five* for February, 1885.

"During the night a few tents had been pitched for the wounded and sick in a hollow behind our position, screened, as we hoped, from the ken of the enemy, but they found them out and gave our force much trouble. The story went that they found out all about our position from a prisoner who had escaped from our quarter-guard. (This man, so it was said, had been *tied* to a sentry—the sentry having declared his utter inability to keep awake on the night of the 17th: if I remember rightly, the sentry was tried, but the sentence remitted by Sir Hugh Rose.) Until the sun got hot we had many visitors at our outpost, a general, some colonels and majors, and many small fry. The Commander of the post was very pertinacious in his requests for advice as to what would be the best thing to do under certain contingencies; these questions had the effect, I noticed, of shortening the visits of the seniors. At last came Major Eyre Massey; whether he was field officer on duty or not, I forget, but his answer showed he considered it either a duty or a kindness to answer the young gentleman's enquiries."

"On the blank page of a Forbes' Manual were already traced out the lines of fire from the post, showing where the first graze of the bullet had been noticed—this made the subject easier to discuss. 'I see you can shoot down anything that comes across your front from the time they cross the nullah by the temple marked A, until they cross this high road at B. Now, remember that if by any chance they get guns up to C, you are done and we are done, for they can then fire straight into our camp and enfilade you; keep them out of that, and if you can't, then retire to that knoll behind, and hold it at all hazards. Yes, you're right, you're a long way from · support and from the camp, and I'll get a couple of troopers sent to that knoll and they can bring back news from you; so make yourself snug and sit tight.'

"These words were spoken twenty-six years ago, and may not be quite correctly given, but the impression still is vivid of a cheery, jerky Irish voice giving decided instructions to a boy in a ticklish position. The boy is grey-headed now, but the sound of the voice is easily recalled, and is now, I trust, cheering and directing the many who want it in the Emerald Isle.*

"It was a weary day, the sun beat down upon the stones around us, the breeze was laden with heat and dust. Breakfast of some sort was brought to us, but of tobacco and other comforts we had been long ignorant. The Commander of the Company had been lately at Hythe (indeed he must have been the only *musketry-instructed* officer with the Regiment), a sergeant and three men of the Company had been there with him, so our time was utilised in devising many cunning musketry traps for the enemy. I can recall this officer's horror at a practical result of his theories; he pointed out a temple, and delivered it as his opinion that it was 950 or more yards distant, and that under certain conditions of light, wind, &c., a full sight might possibly take a bullet to a true billet. This was rather doubted, but later in the morning three men were noticed passing this temple, and at this moment the theorist (who was generally known by the men as Mr. Gravity) was testing various distances by firing, and he was pressed to test the distance of this temple: apparently he did not realise at first that it was a living moving target that he was aiming at, for he only muttered 'the wind is against me,' when a shout from the men awoke him to the grim reality that the last of the three men had dropped. His glasses went up, so I could not see the expression of his face, but I don't think he was proud of his shot, for, as young men go, he was not cold-blooded. Alas, for poor human nature! The other two men stopped and turned to their wounded comrade—'to carry him off perhaps?' No, to take off his boots!

---

* At the time these lines were written, Major Massey—as Lord Clarina — was Major-General Commanding the Dublin District.

CAPTURE OF GWALIOR.

"Three days afterwards the men used to take a stroll out that way to have a look at 'the Captain's skeleton'—you may depend upon it the Captain did not; however, his theories were proved of value later in the day.

"About 3 p.m. considerable movement was observable on the heights to our left, and clouds of dust rose from the Lashkar below, and soon the enemy's parties approached the points we had noted down, but a gentle bouquet of four or five bullets soon warned them off. By four o'clock these constant attentions on our part left few rifles in a fit state to be loaded. A note was therefore despatched to the Brigade Major for water to sponge them out, for, as we fancied, they were only foul after thirty-six hours' work. The little water we had with us had been sparingly drunk, for many had to have their heads 'soused' to save them from succumbing to the sun. Several, however, had sunstroke, and more than one poor boy, who had lately joined us, rolled about in agony with the cramp. (Ah me! those Kilmarnock caps with covers or a dirty white towel round them, no wonder we were bald at twenty-five and grey at thirty; try them, gentlemen, on the anniversary of Waterloo on a rocky hill, without water to drink and nothing to smoke!) In vain we searched for water, none came. An hour passed and the enemy's parties became bolder, until at last a battery and escort descended the hill at a trot and began to cross the nullah at A. 'How many rifles are serviceable?' 'Eight,' is the answer. 'Then send our four best shots into the holes we have dug down there, and see that each has a man to load for him.' 'All ready,' was shouted when they were snug.

"'Now fire a volley when they come out of the nullah and form.' Four puffs of smoke, four cracks, and the whole picquet starts up to see the result. A moment's suspense, then a cloud of dust, and it seems to us that at least a horse or two are down. Anyhow, they halt, but here advance three horsemen at a gallop; they are alone. It is evident they want to cross our front, and the caution of Major Massey is recalled—'you are done if they get guns there.' The word is passed to fire no more shots until the horsemen cross the road six hundred yards from us. Then all four rifles are fired, and the two leading men are knocked over. Through the ploughed black soil toils the third man, and as he unhesitatingly approaches the spot where his comrades lie, he bends his head to his saddle bow, and you fancy you can hear the black horse's sobs and the man's breath come and go. Out ring the four rifles followed by genuine cheers from the picquet as the plucky horseman passes unhurt away from our range to the distant hill.

"Well, one has got there safe, and if he gets back to the battery he will tell them what we do not want them to know. He halts, looks calmly round, and turns his horse's head to return, *but by another way!* Meanwhile, heavy firing had been going on near the camp, and all our force had been called out. Soon an order was received for the Company to hold on *at all hazards* to its post, or anyhow to the hillocks behind, and two camels were seen approaching. 'Water at last!' we cried. Alas, *it was ammunition!* Heaven knows we already had more of that than we wanted, as only some five rifles were now serviceable. The last of our water was now distributed, and these men cleaned out their rifles with it instead of drinking it, which struck the writer as showing very great self-denial. But the sun is now sinking, and the danger is, we think, over, for the Commander of that halted battery by the nullah never succeeded in hardening his heart sufficiently to attempt to cross our front; if he had shelled us and then galloped across, I fear our few rifles would not have been of much value. However, we were all very pleased that we had never to budge from our post." (As the relieving company under Brevet-Major Plunkett came up, a round shot knocked over a section of fours, taking off the head of the left hand man, cutting the pouch off the next, broke the thigh of the third, and cut away the calf of the fourth). "And when at ten p.m. we were relieved, we were very particular in explaining to our successors that pluck and clean rifles were all that were requisite to hold the place; but we wanted dinner for ourselves, so we tramped back to camp with visions of a mess tent, tea, and food of sorts, only to find some twenty sleeping forms which grunted when you asked questions; finally, our hopes were quenched in a draught of cold water, which the Roman Catholic Priest, Mr. Strickland, kindly got for us. Thus closed the 18th June.

"'Let the boy sleep, he is dead tired,' were the first words I heard as I came to semi-consciousness soon after daylight on the 19th June; there seemed to be a busy hum of voices round me, some of them familiar, and after a time I realised that Sir Hugh Rose and his staff were with us; before they moved away I had an opportunity of asking one of his staff, whom I had known before, what was going to be done. 'Well, I can tell you what is intended to be done; we are to bridge that water-course you came across on the 17th, and make a road over this nullah, then cross the hill opposite to-morrow, and thence attack the town; meantime, we shall send our cavalry round to the east of the fortress and catch them in a net; on the third day the Union Jack is to wave over the fortress. That is our intention, but my impression is that Gwalior will be ours by sunset to day.

"So, covering and working parties, furnished by the 86th Regiment, were sent down to the nullah, and for a time it seemed as if we were to have a quiet morning; by and by, however, the covering parties seemed to be spoiling for a fight, and a shot here and there soon increased into an occasional volley. 'Shall we reinforce the covering parties,' was asked of Sir Hugh. 'Certainly not,' was the answer, 'if they are reinforced they will advance and bring on a general engagement—the very thing I want to avoid.'

"Easy in my mind on hearing this, I betook me to the shady side of a recumbent camel, and went to sleep. I do not know how long I slept, but I was disturbed by hearing the 95th 'call' sound, and the order for the left wing to fall in; an hour later, two or three more companies fell in and were soon followed by us. By the time we crossed the nullah, we found the whole force marching along the crest of the hills, which ran in a semicircle to our left front from our camp towards the Lashkar. We were the rearmost company of the array; below us in the basin to our right front, were scattered bodies of the enemy rapidly disappearing towards the city; we passed some guns, lately belonging to the enemy, being worked by Lieutenant Brockman, of the 86th, Lieutenant Budgen, 95th, our Adjutant, Lieutenant Sexton, and some others; a mishap occurred to some ammunition, and, besides other casualties, I remember Lieutenant Sexton was terribly burnt. A request to permit our company to go off to the low ground to our right was granted by Major Vialls, who was at the moment in command, for he saw there was a chance for us to do some work; but we were cautioned against the enemy's cavalry who were still hovering around, but these appeared to be far more cautious of us, for after a few shots we found ourselves enabled to push on and do rather a good stroke of business, *viz.*, to locate ourselves on the right and most advanced knoll of the position held by Sir Hugh Rose's forces, for as they traversed the semicircle of hills we nipped across the arc. Of course, we had had to hurry a bit, and we were glad to lie down and rest when we reached our goal. We found two 18-pounder guns concealed by some trees some thousand or twelve hundred yards from us, and these occasionally knocked up the dust around us. Colonel Raines was not displeased, I think, at finding that a portion of the Regiment had slipped from the tail of the force to the head of it: he was, however, firm in refusing us permission to attack the two guns until he could support us with cavalry.

"Those who remember—who does not?—Lieut.-Colonel Norton Knatchbull, can easily picture to themselves the senior subaltern of No. 1 Company, as he stood in that June sun; a black velvet hunting-cap covered with a towel, a torn canvas coat ornamented by a ragged sash—with the usual ragged blue trousers and a small remnant of boots.* But he was 6ft. 2in., as strong as Wiltshire Downs could make him, with a voice like a gong; added to this, he was, at that time, probably the fastest runner in the British Army—to him was deputed the duty of trying to get up a howitzer and tumbril, that were lying some three hundred yards below us, towards the enemy; it had been hastily abandoned, but the bullocks were still there. Knatchbull took eight or ten unarmed men with him, while we kept up a smart fire on the enemy to cover the adventure. It is difficult to say which was the most disagreeable—the enemy's fire or the conduct of their cattle, for the bullocks of '57 had the same dislike to a white face as we find to be the case now; they for a time defended the gun nobly, but eventually, breaking away, galloped off to the enemy. This was embarrassing, but the brawny men of No. 1 laid on with a will, and soon we had our artillery in position. Now we found a new difficulty; deeply versed in the theory and practice of rifle shooting as Mr. Gravity undoubtedly was, he hesitated when he was asked for directions how to load the gun; luckily, a Militia Artillery recruit had joined us a few days before, and he took charge of his novel Infantry weapon. By this time, the force had become

---

*Colonel Knatchbull says:—"I marched into Gwalior wearing one boot and one shoe—the former a present from Major Vialls—the one much too large, the other far too small"!!

aware of what we were up to, and had rewarded our
late escapade with a cheer, and looked, with curiosity
no doubt, for our next move. I always considered
that we did very well, for although the first shell
burst about fiteen yards from the muzzle, yet we had
not expected it to burst at all, and we were as much
pleased with this result as could be expected, when
we remembered the distance we were from the
bursting shell. Number Two round burst about three
hundred yards beyond the enemy's 18-pounders, and
certainly very high up, but I have no doubt its moral
effect was very great. (I am bound to say that, so
far, only sounds of laughter travelled to us from the
recumbent battalion on our left, but this changed to a
shout when Number Three burst just over the guns.)
But no more time for long bowls, Colonel Raines now
gave us permission to take the guns, as a squadron of
the Bombay Lancers was at hand to support us; all I
can say is, that if the way in which they supported
us, is the usual assistance given to charging Infantry
by Cavalry, I should prefer less support! It was a
narrow road deep in dust, we charged in columns of
sections, and when, within sixty or seventy yards of
the guns, these blue-coated troopers charged through
us, the writer, who was as small then as now, was
knocked over, but was at once picked up and put on
the shoulders of two men with the remark—'We'll not
leave the little officer behind'—and truly they did
not, and after a dusty hustle I found myself on one
of the guns. Norton Knatchbull was lying across its
breach, panting, and white with dust. It was a vexed
point as to who took the guns, but Knatchbull was
the first of ours in, and he it was who, if I remember
rightly, scratched '95' on one of the guns with his
sword. As soon as we had pulled ourselves together,
the cavalry were taken off to the right, while the infantry battalions poured down the hills on to the city.
Sir Hugh Rose came up, and, preceded by a section of
No. 1, entered the streets of the city at the head

CAPTURE OF GWALIOR. 45

of the Force; he rode along quite calmly as if it were down Piccadilly on a summer afternoon, instead of a captured city with gentlefolks firing out of the upper stories. No. 1 Company of the 95th were thus the vanguard of the army which entered Gwalior city that afternoon of the 19th June, 1858. We did not see the remainder of the Regiment until, I think, the 20th or 21st; that night we were lodged by the Maharaja Scindiah in his palace, and daintily fed on champagne and cooked meats of sorts. Thus ended the three days' adventures of No. 1 Company before Gwalior, and the prophecy of the morning turned out to be true, that before sundown the city would be ours."

(Lieutenant Knatchbull—with whom were Ensigns Fawcett and Wilkinson—commanded the guard left in the Palace.)

Meanwhile, the 95th Regiment had paraded soon after breakfast in their shirt sleeves, and with cooked rations in their haversacks; shortly after nine o'clock news was received from the vedettes that a large body of men was seen to debouch from Gwalior, accompanied by cavalry and fresh guns, and was ascending the heights to reinforce the battery on the ridge, on the same level as our camping ground, and about a mile and a half to our left front; this was good news for us, as the more guns the rebels brought up on to the heights, the more we were likely to capture. At the same time, express news came from the front that the Sepoys were mustering strong on our left flank, with the object of attacking us at noon, the hottest part of the day, in the hope that the sun would favour their operations; they seemed inclined not to confine their advance to an affair of outposts, but to be determined to attack the flank—which they knew was weak—vigorously. It was therefore ordered that the 86th Regiment, commanded by Lieut.-Colonel Louth, should move across the canal, supported by the 25th Bombay Infantry under Captain Pelly, and, crowning the heights on the other side, attack the enemy on their left front; to divert attention from this movement, Lieut.-Colonel Raines was directed to move with the 95th from the right front across the canal, over the shoulder of the hill (on which was the rebel battery) against the enemy's left flank. This oblique movement and the lie of the ground prevented the 95th from suffering from the fire of the battery: the 10th Bombay Infantry, under Captain Roome, four hundred yards on the right rear, supported the steady advance of the 95th. Just on crowning the hill the 95th came to close quarters with the enemy, who, perceiving themselves to be taken in flank, retired rapidly towards their battery. The skirmishers of the 86th pressed the rebel infantry so hard that they did not make a stand even under their guns, but retreated across the entrenchment in rear. The gallant 86th gave them no time to rally, but dashing at the parapet with a cheer, captured the three brass guns defending the ridge. Lieutenant Brockman of the 86th, and Lieutenants Budgen and Sexton of the 95th, were placed in charge of these guns, which were turned against the enemy and made excellent practice. It was while serving these guns that Lieutenant and Adjutant Sexton was nearly blown to pieces by an explosion of powder, and was so severely burnt that he had to retire to camp, but not until he had been compelled to do so by Assistant-Surgeon Clarke of the 95th. Lieut.-Colonel Raines, too, was here severely wounded by a musket ball in the left arm, but he continued in command of the Regiment.

The 95th then advanced a quarter of a mile towards Gwalior to the crest of the slope that commanded the Phul Bagh or Lashkar, the Grand Parade Ground of the Gwalior Maharaja's troops, where the enemy was gathered in force with two 18-pounders. It was here that Lieutenant Knatchbull manned the howitzer and turned it on the clusters of the enemy in front.

No. 2 Company was also on outpost duty this morning, and when the chain of sentries had been posted, the officers sat down behind a low "sangar" or dry stone wall. As the enemy's shots were constantly whistling over this position one of the officers got up and put a few big stones on the top of the wall to make it high enough to protect their heads; he then resumed his breakfast. On going round to revisit his men, he noticed a star made by a bullet on one of the very stones that he had placed on the top of the wall. Just as this party had been relieved and was formed up preparatory to marching back to camp, a shell pitched into the middle of them, taking off the leg of a man of the 95th named Nelson, and wounding others. Indeed, the enemy continued to fire all that day, but chiefly with round shot. These came into the little hollow where our few tents were pitched and appeared so harmless, as they bounded down the slope like a cricket ball, that some of the men were with difficulty prevented from trying to "field" them! The force with which these round shot were going was of course enormous, although they appeared to go so slowly.

The shooting on our side was now so hot that soon the rebel gunners left their guns and ran for shelter behind the neighbouring houses, occasionally, however, the gunners popped out from behind their cover to load and fire their 18-pounders. Some of the mutineer gunners stood to their guns with astonishing pluck, and in one case they remained serving a gun until every man was hit—the last man of the detachment working his gun entirely by himself for fully ten minutes before he was struck down.

After remaining half-an-hour on the crest of the hill—the 95th lying down in line to escape the shot and rest the men—the remainder of the 95th, under Major Vialls, joined the right wing in support.

The enemy were now seen in force occupying the houses amongst the trees, and firing on the skirmishers of the 86th Regiment, who were steadily advancing in that direction, so Captain E. D. Smith's Company of the 95th was ordered to proceed in support of the 86th and so became detached from the Regiment. On a spur running down parallel to the entrenchments, some forty or fifty rebels were under cover in different spots, and were firing at our men, who, exposed in the open, were serving the captured guns; it was now that the 10th Bombay Infantry, under Captain Roome, joined the 95th, and a portion of the 10th were pushed on to support the 95th skirmishers in front; the rest of the 10th occupied the spur and drove the enemy further into the Lashkar, capturing a small brass howitzer and also a mortar abandoned by the enemy. Captain Roome was ordered to send on part of a Company to disable the guns by knocking off a wheel. At this time two Companies of the 95th were at the bottom of the hill in skirmishing order, firing lying down, with two other Companies and the rest of the 10th a hundred yards in rear awaiting orders. Just at this moment Sir Hugh Rose rode up with his staff, and highly praised the 95th for their gallant behaviour; Lieut.-Colonel Raines suggested to Sir Hugh that he should take No. 1 Company and capture the enemy's two heavy guns, to which he replied: "Yes, do so, and I will support you with a troop of the Bombay Lancers." The guns were captured as before recorded. The subsequent advance through the city was by no means without danger, as a few desperate men were met with who reserved their fire until the head of the Column reached them. Lieutenant Mills, Bombay Lancers, was shot dead by such a man, who rushed out of a house and fired at him from within a few inches. After the taking of the city, three Companies of the 95th remained on picquet duty at the Maharajah's Palace for the night, and the rest of the battalion reached camp about eight p.m.

Abandoning the defence of Gwalior, while his

troops were still fighting, Tantia Topee, with a considerable body of cavalry and infantry, attempted to retreat northwards, but learning that Punniar was already occupied by the British, he went to the Residency, where the rest of the rebel army joined him in the retreat from Gwalior, due north to Alipore.

The following officers and men of the 95th were favourably mentioned by Sir Hugh Rose for good and gallant service during the four days, from the 16th to the 19th June:—

- Lieut.-Colonel Raines, Commanding H.M.'s 95th Regiment (two special mentions), in gallantly and ably commanding H.M.'s 95th Regiment when they took the heights on the ridge above Gwalior, and captured two pieces of artillery. Good service in turning the captured guns on the enemy, and taking by assault two eighteen-pounders on the Grand Parade of Gwalior.
- Major Vialls, H.M.'s 95th Regiment (special mention), good service for taking the extreme right of a spur of the last and lowest height above Gwalior.
- Lieutenant Budgen and Lieutenant and Adjutant Sexton, H.M.'s 95th Regiment (mention), ably serving captured guns.
- Lieutenant Knatchbull, H.M.'s 95th Regiment (mention), for with some men of his company removing a howitzer, and turning it on the enemy.
- Dr. Clarke H.M.'s 95th Regiment (mention), attendance on sick and wounded.
- Privates P. Murphy, Loix, Dempsey and Colville, H.M.'s 95th Regiment (mention), ably serving captured guns.

For these services Lieut.-Colonel Raines received the C.B. and was promoted Brevet-Colonel; Majors Vialls and Massey received Brevet-Lieut.-Colonelcies; and Captain Foster was promoted to a Brevet-Majority

The following were the casualties in the 95th Regiment in the four days' fighting:—

Killed: Private Joseph Shaw.
Wounded: Lieutenant-Colonel Raines, Lieutenants Crealock and Sexton, Corporal Hunt, Privates Bird, Cole, Dutton, Hall, Hogan, Johnson, McCartney, Nelson, Pike, Robinson, Rodden, Suttle and Swan.

CHAPTER IV.

ACTIONS OF POWREE, BEEJAPORE AND KOONDRYE; CLOSE OF THE CAMPAIGN.

THE rock-fortress of Gwalior was, however, still in possession of the enemy; a Force of cavalry, with horse artillery, was sent out in pursuit of the rebels, and these were again defeated by Colonel Napier, afterwards Lord Napier of Magdala, at a place called Alipore, and completely routed.

On the morning of the 24th June, a grand review was held on the Morar plain of all the troops under the command of Sir Hugh Rose, on which occasion two out of every three men of the 95th went past barefooted, the Regiment having by then marched 1800 miles and left behind all supplies and stores. On the afternoon of the same day the fortress was assaulted and captured. The Maharaja Scindiah was so grateful to the Force for having so successfully fought for him and for having replaced him on the throne, that he petitioned to be allowed to present six months' batta as well as a special decoration to every man, but the request was declined by the Government of India on the ground of "want of precedent."

Very soon after the capture of Gwalior, the monsoon, which was long overdue, commenced, and the old cavalry stables and huts in which the 95th were temporarily accommodated, were inundated with water. These buildings were also extremely dirty and this caused a good deal of sickness, indeed it is probable that if the Regiment had remained at Gwalior throughout the monsoon, few of the men would have been fit for service afterwards; but as it was found that the Mutiny was not yet fully crushed, the Regiment was ordered out into the field again and marched for Seepree. The country for part of the way was literally under water, but the soil being gravelly and the air pure, the health of the Battalion rapidly improved.

On the 20th July, the 95th accordingly left Gwalior for Seepree, about eight days' march distant, where the Regiment hoped to enjoy some well-earned repose, and where the men at once began building huts. However, here the Regiment rejoined Brigadier Michael Smith's Brigade and marched on the 6th August, without tents or kits, against Powree, a fortified village some twenty miles north-west of Seepree, which had shortly before been captured by the rebel chief, Man Singh. On arrival before the town, it was found to be defended by a strong bastioned wall mounting many guns, and as the Brigade had no siege artillery with it—nor, indeed, was there any nearer than Gwalior—it became necessary to fall back and bivouac within sight of the place until guns could be brought up to demolish the stone-built fortifications. On the 19th August, Brigadier-General Sir Robert Napier arrived with a siege train and reinforcements of infantry, and on the following day the siege began—the fort being shelled for two days and nights. Owing to the weakness of the besieging force and the extent of the place, the town could only be partially invested; consequently, on the night of the 21st-22nd, the enemy escaped by the unprotected side, and shortly before a breaching battery (which had been finished during the early part of the night) was to have opened fire. On the following morning the 95th formed part of the Column of pursuit which was sent after the fugitives, and which, after a forced march of twenty-five miles, came up with two brass field guns which had been abandoned. Night coming

[To face page 58.

on now put an end to the pursuit, and the Column returned to Powree the next day.

On the 21st August, Lieutenant Fisher and Private McHale had been severely wounded—the former through the chest. Fisher and other officers were reconnoitring the enemy from the top of a native house about four hundred yards from the walls of the town. There was a low parapet about two feet high behind which they sat, resting their field-glasses upon it and watching and recording the movements of the enemy. Fisher got up, and turning round, walked to a doorway in a higher part of the house and a few yards from him; as he reached it, he exclaimed, " I am shot "! A large oval Lancaster bullet had struck him in the shoulder-blade and had passed straight through him, making an enormous wound and striking the wall behind him. He was immediately attended to by the regimental surgeon, but he never lost consciousness, and half an hour afterwards was able to talk, and said that he " didn't feel very bad." He recovered perfectly.

The night before the assault was to have taken place, Lieut. J. N. Crealock, with one sergeant and twelve privates of the Light Company—all volunteers —reconnoitred the ground between the breaching battery, above referred to, and the intended breach, for which service they were mentioned by Sir R. Napier in his despatch reporting the operations. Major Vialls volunteered to remain in command of the advanced post during the siege, and was mentioned in the despatch, while Lieutenants Budgen and Pearson and Ensign Anderson acted as Assistant Field Engineers, and were likewise mentioned.

The bulk of the 95th Regiment returned to Seepree on the 31st August, after destroying the greater part of the fortifications of Powree; but as the garrison was known to have consisted of some of the most guilty and formidable of the mutineers, who still kept the field, a pursuing Column was immediately organised, consisting of detachments from the 8th Hussars, 95th Regiment, and 10th Bombay Native Infantry—the infantry on camels—the whole under Lieutenant-Colonel Robertson, of the 25th Native Infantry. This Force at once started in pursuit, and for ten days and nights continued its march through dense jungle, halting at night, and marching from dawn to sunset, with only very short halts for food. Touch with the enemy was never lost, and information of their doings was daily received, but they were equally well informed of our movements, and succeeded in keeping beyond our reach. The troops were now becoming exhausted, so Colonel Robertson prepared a small and carefully selected party, consisting of one squadron of the 8th Hussars, one company of the 95th, under Captain Foster—with whom were Lieutenant Fawcett and Ensign Wilkinson—and seventy of the 10th Native Infantry. All weakly men were left behind, together with a company of the 10th Native Infantry. This Force then commenced a day-and-night forced march, halting only when absolutely necessary for food and short periods of rest. Forty miles were accomplished in twenty-six hours, and on the 5th September, before daybreak, the men became aware that they were approaching the bivouac of the enemy, estimated to be about five hundred strong. They were sleeping on a small patch of rising ground, just beyond the village of Beejapore; the Parbuttee River—a stream of considerable size—ran past the village and along the foot of this small eminence. The whole of the surrounding country was composed of rather unusually thick jungle with small patches of cultivation near the village, which was more or less shaded by some lofty trees, in the branches of which roosted large numbers of pea-fowl. These were the first to notice our quiet advance and did their best, by their continuous screaming, to alarm the enemy.

The squadron of the 8th Hussars had sometime

previously been sent round, by a long detour, to cut off the enemy's retreat.

The Company of the 95th led the attack, and advanced as silently as possible past the flank of the village of Beejapore, and on leaving it to their right rear came into full sight of the rising ground where the enemy were sleeping. The dawn was just breaking and a few figures could be seen moving leisurely about preparing the morning meal. Suddenly they became aware that they were being attacked, either from hearing the movements of the Hussars, or possibly from the news being conveyed to them from the village, but in a surprisingly short space of time the whole rebel force was on the move and rushing down towards the river.

The infantry of our Force formed to its front, and fired several volleys at a range which could not have exceeded two or three hundred yards. As the sabres of the 8th Hussars could now be seen against the sky-line, firing had to cease and the pursuit was taken up with the bayonet. The broken and wooded nature of the ground soon destroyed all formation, and the pursuit was carried on by groups of men under officers or non-commissioned officers. Very many of the enemy were killed on their camping ground, and still more of them on the banks of the river, but the pursuit was continued till the sun was high in the sky. Soon after crossing the river, Lieutenant Fawcett—whilst pressing through some thick jungle with a few men in pursuit of a large group of mutineers, still in shreds of uniform—was shot through the body and killed instantly. A more promising officer, or one who was more deeply and sincerely mourned by all who knew him, never entered the service.

Gradually the troops returned from the pursuit, and it is computed that four hundred and fifty rebels were left dead on the field, exclusive of those who were drowned in the river. The killed were nearly al

Sepoys of the old Bengal army, and many wore medals. Besides Lieutenant Fawcett, the 95th detachment had Privates O'Keefe mortally, Williams dangerously, and Parsons severely wounded. The 10th had three men killed and four wounded, while the 8th Hussars had both their officers, Poore and Hanbury, and their sergeant-major, Champion, wounded.

The remnant of the enemy dispersed into the jungle, and were never heard of again as a formed body.

The officer and private of the 95th were buried under a tree on rising ground near the scene of action and close to the river. Twenty years afterwards a solid bronze recumbent cross, with a suitable inscription, was placed over the grave, and when the village was visited for this purpose it was found that the natives had—unasked—taken the most scrupulous care of the grave during the whole preceding twenty years, and it was as perfect and well cared for as any of their own sacred shrines. They stated that during the action of Beejapore and subsequent pursuit of the enemy, seventeen men of their own village had, in mistake, been killed.

Captain Foster was honorably mentioned in the despatch describing the action of Beejapore.

By this time the rebel Tantia Topee was on his way back to Central India, but shortly after the action at Beejapore he was overtaken and routed by General Michel at Rajghar, but, worsted and hunted as he was, he remained in force threatening Seronge and Chundaree. Smith's brigade—including the 95th Regiment—was engaged in the pursuit, which now commenced; the brigade marched to Esaughur, only to find that the place had been evacuated by the rebels the day before; and the efforts subsequently made to capture Tantia Topee proving unsuccessful, Smith's brigade was left in October, after many long marches, to watch the different fords of the Betwa river from Seronge to prevent the escape southwards

ACTION OF BEEJAPORE.

of Tantia Topee and Ferozeshah. Tantia Topee, however, fled into Nimar and marched into Guzerat, so that once again it seemed as though nothing remained for the Brigade to do. It accordingly left Seronge, having several skirmishes in the jungle there, and proceeded to Goona, dispersing and destroying on its road the band of rebels who followed Man Singh, the same who had shortly before been driven from his stronghold at Powree. Hardly, however, had the Brigade reached Goona, when the inroad of the rebel Ferozeshah, backed by a large body of followers, took place, and again the Brigade had to take the field. It returned to Seronge on the Grand Trunk Road—a central and commanding position—but though it failed to meet with Ferozeshah, who was afterwards soundly beaten at Runnod by Sir Robert Napier, the Brigade succeeded in destroying or dispersing many of his followers at Baroda and Arrone. Soon after, Tantia Topee and Ferozeshah were able to effect a junction of their forces, and the Brigade was again obliged to make long marches; it advanced to the Chumbul, crossed that river in pursuit, followed the rebels across the Banas, and eventually pursued them as far as Tonk on the borders of Bikaneer; and so closely were the pursuers treading on the heels of the enemy, that the Brigade often reached a camping ground only a few hours after it had been vacated, and found the fires still smouldering.

Again, the two rebel chiefs doubled back, and made their way for the third time to Central India and the Seronge jungles, closely followed by Smith's Brigade, which was at last able to inflict such a defeat upon them, that they were finally crippled and obliged to flee northwards, with only a remnant of their following. The Brigade then received orders to march southward along the Grand Trunk Road, scouring the jungles on either side, until, on the evening of the 11th November, when in camp at Godowlie, information was received that the rebels

were in the neighbourhood, and orders were issued for
the Force to be in readiness to move at a moment's
notice. The troops left camp on the 13th, at 4.30
a.m., and marched as far as Bakkapoor, then turned
in the direction of a village where Man Singh was
said to be, and here a halt was made for breakfast.
On moving forward once more, a cloud of dust in the
distance showed that the enemy was on the wing:
pursuit was kept up until sunset, traces of the rebels'
flight being everywhere quite fresh. Pursuit was
resumed next morning at 4 a.m., information having
come in that the enemy had doubled back to a
village called Koondrye, where they were said to be
sleeping quite unconscious of the proximity of their
pursuers. After the column had marched for about
an hour and a half, the camp fires were sighted, and
the attack was at once arranged.

The Bombay Lancers were sent off to the right, the
guns and 8th Hussars to the left, while an extended
company of the 95th, supported by another and by two
of the 10th, formed the centre. The rest of the Force
followed in column in rear of the left and centre. The
enemy was taken completely by surprise, the 95th
advanced in line, the cavalry getting quickly to work
on the flanks among the enemy who offered but slight
resistance; the pursuit was continued for nearly five
miles to the village of Rajpoor where the force
bivouacked. The loss of the rebels was estimated
at close upon six hundred *killed*. In this action
Captain Harris, of the Bombay Horse Artillery, was
shot through the arm, and it was at first thought that
the shot had been fired by a man of the 95th;
however, Captain Stockwell turning round, happened
to see some smoke coming from a bush, and, rushing
up, discovered a rebel hiding behind it armed with
a sword and a musket which he was in the act of
re-loading, when Captain Stockwell ran him through
the body with his sword.

A few days before this action, Lieutenant-Colonel

ACTION OF KOONDRYE.

Hon. F. Thesiger had joined the 95th as second in command, on exchange with Lieutenant-Colonel Hume, and he commanded the infantry of the Brigade during the day; Lieutenant-Colonel Raines commanded the 95th, while Lieutenant A. M. Rawlins was employed as orderly officer to the Brigadier; all these three officers were mentioned by Brigadier Smith in his despatch for their services during the action. This was the last engagement in which the 95th Regiment—as a whole—took part in Central India, and on this occasion one man—Private William Brooks—was wounded, receiving a severe sword-cut in the wrist.

However, although the 95th—as a battalion—was not again engaged, detachments of the corps still did much good work, while even the various drafts of recruits, which arrived in India from England to join the service companies, were constantly and successfully employed in the field against the rebels.

The following drafts had arrived in India and either joined the service companies or the depôt, which was located first at Deesa and afterwards at Neemuch; in February, 1858, Lieutenant Gabbett arrived in India accompanied by one sergeant and forty rank and file; in April, 102 rank and file reached Bombay; in October, 106; and in November, seventy-four rank and file. Two drafts of fifty-eight and of twenty-five rank and file respectively also reached India from England in January and February, 1859.

A party of one sergeant and twenty privates of the 95th, who accompanied a column under Sir John Michel, composed principally of cavalry and horse artillery, was present at the actions of Sandwaho and Kownee, on the 19th and 25th October respectively, when the rebels under Tantia Topee were defeated with great loss. The following detachments of recruits, &c., belonging to the 95th, were also actively engaged in the field against the enemy previous to their joining the service companies; viz., on the 24th December, 1858, the detachment stationed at Neemuch accompanied a field force from that station sent in pursuit of the rebels under Tantia Topee, and was present under command of Captain Brooke at the action of Pertabghur, where the enemy was defeated with loss; this detachment soon afterwards marched from Neemuch and joined Headquarters in Central India; another detachment of over 200, under Captain Benison, operated with a column under Major Chetwode, 8th Hussars, in Central India, and also under Colonel Rich in the Muksoodenghur jungles. A third detachment of recruits over a hundred strong, under Lieutenant Bonnor-Maurice, also operated in Central India, and was present with Major Chetwode's force at the demolishing of the fort of Narghar. Besides this, the several drafts of the Regiment forwarded from Bombay, from time to time, to reinforce the Headquarter companies, did good service *en route*, having been frequently employed, in conjunction with other troops, in pursuit of the rebels and in defending passes and fords, whereby the enemy might have escaped into the Southern Mahratta country; this was an event much to be guarded against, as, though hitherto this district had not openly risen in rebellion against us, it was known to be ripe for revolt.

On the 26th November, the Regiment halted at Seronge, remaining there nearly a week, and on the 29th the Queen's Proclamation was read out on a "strong as possible" parade, in English and in the vernacular, and on the same occasion medals for "long service and good conduct" were presented to Colour-Sergeant Garrett and to Private Dempsey.

On the 15th December, the depôt, families, baggage, &c., which had been left at Deesa the preceding January, arrived at Neemuch and joined the detachment under Captain Langford-Brooke, which had already been quartered at that station for some considerable time; while on the 24th February a detachment under Lieutenant-Colonel Hon. F. A. Thesiger, consisting of seven officers and two hundred rank and file, marched from Tonk for Nusseerabad.

Towards the end of March, only a small party of the 95th still kept the field, and was in the vicinity of Muksoodenghur; the enemy were reported to be only some seven miles off, and of a strength of 1500; the thermometer in the hospital tent stood at 100 degrees, and the *second* hot weather spent in the field was coming on apace.

On the 31st March the small force marched at three a.m.—having been already once roused earlier in the night—about a mile in the direction of the enemy, when some scouts ran in, reporting that the rebels were already on the move, whereupon our force turned about, and went back to camp. A sowar, who had been sent with a message to another force, which was operating in the neighbourhood, under Colonel Rich, was killed by the enemy, and his body left upon the road. Colonel Rich sent over a hundred and fifty trotting camels, and ninety men of the 95th and fifty of the 10th Bombay Infantry, were formed into a Camel Corps, of which Captain Carmichael was put in command, with Lieutenants Bacon and Gabbett as his subalterns. On the 1st April, the 8th Hussars and the Camel Corps, under Major Massey, marched at 1 a.m. to a village called Jinseah, some nine miles distant, arriving there just before daybreak, the road being very stony and through dense jungle. On approaching the village a number of lights were seen, but these turned out to be the smouldering remains of the village itself, which had been burnt two days previously by Mayne's Irregulars. The Hussars were now sent home, there being no water for their horses, but the rest of the force remained all day in the neighbourhood, as the spies in the service of Captain Bolton, A.Q.M.G. for Intelligence, had been ordered to meet him here. However, the bulk of the Force shortly drew off, leaving a small party, under Lieutenant Bacon, to bring in the spies. The first party reached camp about sunset, that under Bacon about 9 p.m.

The Force was roused up at 2.30 on the morning of the 3rd, as an attempt to surprise a body of the rebels —who were said to be in the jungles some nine miles east of Muksoodenghur—had been decided upon. The Force was divided into two portions. Colonel De Salis took the 8th Hussars, the Camel Corps, and a company each of the 95th (under Captain Parkinson) and 10th Native Infantry; the rest of the Column, with two Horse Artillery guns, was sent about nine miles to the south of Muksoodenghur, where it was to halt. After about an hour's delay, caused by the receipt of intelligence that Tantia Topee, with a large following, was only about six miles off in another direction, the Force under De Salis moved off, and reached about sunrise the place where they had expected to find the enemy. These, however, had moved to the westward, and were seen, as the British retraced their steps, at a village at the base of the hills along which our party was retiring. Our skirmishers were at once extended, and sweeping the jungle, moved down upon the village, the 8th Hussars at the same time turning down to the plain. The village was, however, found to be unoccupied, the inhabitants stating that the enemy had passed through only about a quarter of an hour before, without halting.

Whilst halting here, the scouts brought in word that the baggage of the Main Column had been attacked: on return to camp, De Salis' Force was itself attacked—but by swarms of *bees*, the rebels having disturbed these wild bees on their march; several of the men were so badly stung that they were in hospital for several days.

On arrival in camp it was found that the report of the attack on the baggage was correct. It appeared that the rebels, disturbed by us when retreating westward, had come across our baggage which was moving south; they had but a short time for plunder, but they cut down and murdered a Mr. Molta, the civilian Bandmaster of the 10th Native Infantry, and several officers' servants. Sergeant Bramley, the hospital sergeant of the 95th, opened fire upon the enemy, and the baggage guard doubling up to the scene, the rebels were driven off. Their movements, however, were carefully and closely watched, and they did not long escape punishment for their attack upon our baggage, sick, and followers. On the night of the 4th April, in consequence of information received, the Force under Colonel De Salis set out, and arrived at the village of Boorda, near which the enemy was reported to be harbouring, about an hour and a half before daybreak. A company of the 95th and one of the 10th Native Infantry extended in skirmishing order, the rest of the Column—with the cavalry in rear of all—being held in reserve. The Force moved for some time through the dark jungle in this order, and the men were beginning to fear that it was going to be another "blank day," when Captain Bolton caught sight of the rebel camp some sixty yards in front. Just as a halt was made to examine the position carefully,—"bang" went a shot from one of our skirmishers, thus betraying our presence!

There was nothing for it but to rush the camp, which was done with the greatest enthusiasm—skirmishers, reserve, and cavalry all rushing to the front as fast as two deep nullahs and the dense jungle would permit. The enemy bolted at once, but our men were too close for a good many of them, and the pursuit was continued for at least two miles, upwards of three hundred mutineers—among them one Chattar Singh, a noted leader—being killed and a large number of prisoners taken. A great many of the fugitives fled past Major Massey's party at Jinseah, where several more were cut up; while Colonel Rich's Column fell in with many more and accounted for nearly a hundred of the rebels who had taken refuge in a village. Our loss in the affair at Boorda was only one Sepoy wounded.

Major Hon. E. Massey and Captain Carmichael, of the 95th, were mentioned for their services in these operations.

Soon after the 15th April, the camels of the Camel Corps were handed over to Colonel Rich's Column, and shortly after, this detachment of the 95th rejoined Headquarters.

It was not long before Tantia Topee, who had hidden himself in an old temple in the jungle, was surrounded by a party of Meade's Horse, and was captured, tried, and hanged.

About the end of February, Brigadier Michael Smith, who had commanded the Brigade for the past twelve months, had broken down in health, and had been invalided to Bombay, Colonel De Salis, 8th Hussars, assuming the command of the Brigade.

At Jamnair, on the 28th April, the Brigade was at last broken up, and the various regiments composing it left camp for summer quarters; but before marching, the Brigadier—De Salis—issued a farewell order, of which the following is an extract: "The Brigade is about to march to cantonments, and the Commanding Officer congratulates the officers, non-commissioned officers and privates on the termination of their long-continued exertions, which he trusts deserve well of their Queen and Country. Since operations commenced, the regiments forming the Brigade have marched nearly 3000 miles, have been engaged fourteen times with the enemy, and have served under the Generals of four Divisions, each of whom has called for fresh and more arduous exertions. It is not for Colonel de Salis to say how these calls have been responded to, but he may say that it was impossible for any body of men to have evinced more military discipline and subordination, more zeal

CLOSE OF THE CAMPAIGN.

or untiring goodwill, or a better spirit whenever their enemies were before them."

In the beginning of May the weather was oppressively sultry, and the hot season had commenced in earnest, but still the men marched on cheerily, and on the 12th May the 95th Regiment, led by Colonel Raines on his grey Arab, strode into cantonments at a swinging pace, headed by "Derby the First," the prisoner of Kotah, their band playing the well-known strains of "I'm Ninety-five," with their bugle, fife and drum band twenty-eight strong under Drum-Major McDowell. The sick list just then was a heavy one, for there were two officers and seventy-six men unable to march, laid up with guinea-worm, supposed to have been contracted in the Tonk jheels. The hardships and privations which all ranks had endured in the past two years of continual marching and fighting, and under privations of all sorts, had greatly injured the constitutions of many, so much so that land scurvy broke out in the regiment, but being early detected by Assistant-Surgeon Clark, vigorous measures were adopted to check its ravages, and but few men fell victims to it.

Neemuch was found to be in ruins, having been destroyed by the rebels, and the men of the 95th had hard work to get roofs over their heads before the first burst of the monsoon. The detachment under Lieutenant-Colonel the Hon. F. Thesiger, from Nusseerabad, had already reached Neemuch, as had also the depôt of four officers and about a hundred men from Mount Abu and Deesa. Within a week of the arrival of the Battalion, Captain Benison's detachment also joined Head-quarters, so that the whole Regiment was at last concentrated for the first time since embarkation at Kingstown nearly two years before.

* * * *

From the records in the India Office it appears that *three* medal rolls were submitted for the medal, and that these contained the names of 777 individuals; viz., 752 on the first list, 24 names on the second, and 1 name on the third; of these 777 names, 39 were those of officers, 40 of sergeants, 30 of corporals, 19 of drummers, while 649 were those of private soldiers.

When, however, on the 2nd August, 1861, at Poona, the medals with clasps for "Central India," were presented to the 95th Regiment by General Sir William Mansfield, K.C.B.—then Commander-in-Chief in Bombay—only 14 officers and 527 men were thus decorated.

APPENDIX A.

Roll and Records of Service of the Officers who served in the Central India Campaign in the 95th (The Derbyshire) Regiment.

N.B.—The letters R.W. and L.W. after a name signify that the officer embarked with the Right or Left Wing.

| 1
Lieut.-Col.
Henry
Hume,
R.W. | Appointed to the 95th, May, 1835; lieutenant, Dec., 1837; captain, Jan., 1844; major, Dec., 1852; brevet-lieut.-colonel, Dec., 1854; lieut.-colonel commanding, March, 1855. Embarked for Turkey as junior major of the 95th, was present at the Alma (slightly wounded, horse killed), at the repulse of the Russian sortie of the 26th Oct., and at Inkerman (dangerously wounded, horse shot), succeeded to the command of the Regiment and embarked as Commanding Officer for the Cape in June, 1857. Falling sick soon after arrival in India, he left the Regiment in December, 1857, and exchanged on the 3rd April, 1858, to the Grenadier Guards with Captain and Lieut.-Colonel Hon. F. Thesiger.
Awarded the C.B., 5th class of the Legion of Honour, 4th class of the Medjidie, Crimean medal (3 clasps), and Turkish medal. Was recommended by Lieut.-General Sir de Lacy Evans, commanding 2nd Division, for the V.C. "for | Died 19th Aug., 1892, aged 76, was at the time of his death, Ensign of the Yeomen of the Guard. |

	an act of special and useful valour at an important moment at the Alma."	
2 Major Julius Augustus Robert Raines, L.W.	Appointed ensign in the Buffs, Jan., 1842; ensign 95th, May, 1842; lieutenant, April, 1844; captain, April, 1852; brevet-major, April, 1855; major, May, 1857; lieut.-colonel, Nov., 1857; colonel, July, 1858; major-general, Oct., 1871; lieut.-general, Oct., 1877; and general, July, 1881. Embarked for Turkey with the 95th, and was present at the Alma, at the sortie of the 26th Oct., at Inkerman, and at the Tchernaya; was employed as an assistant-royal engineer from October, 1854 to November, 1855, and was wounded in the trenches on the 17th Oct., 1854. Proceeded to India in command of the Left Wing, assumed command of the Regiment in Dec., 1857, and commanded it throughout the Central India Campaign (wounded, despatches), and until November, 1871. Awarded the 5th class of the Medjidie, the Crimean medal (3 clasps), Turkish and Sardinian medals; for Central India the C.B. and medal (1 clasp); awarded in 1878 the pension for "Distinguished service in the field."	Was made a K.C.B. in May, 1893, and has been Col.-in-chief of the Buffs since Sept., 1882.
3 Lieut.-Col. Hon. Frederick A. Thesiger (now Lord Chelmsford).	Appointed lieutenant Rifle Brigade, Dec., 1844; lieutenant Grenadier Guards, Nov., 1845; captain, Dec., 1850; brevet-major, Nov. 1855; captain and lieut.-colonel, August, 1857; lieut.-colonel, 95th Foot, April, 1858; colonel, April, 1863; major-general, November, 1868; lieut.-general, April, 1882; general, December, 1888. Served with the	Appointed Col. Derbyshire Regt., Feb. 1898.

	Grenadier Guards in the Crimean campaign; served with the 95th Foot in the Campaign in Central India; served in Abyssinia as D. A.-G., and in the Kaffir and Zulu wars in command of the Forces. Awarded G. C. B., Crimean medal (1 clasp), Turkish and Sardinian medals, 5th class of the Medjidie, the India medal and clasp, Abyssinian medal and clasp, and African medal and clasp.	
4 Major George Courtney Vialls, R.W.	Appointed to the 95th Jan. 1843; lieutenant, May, 1846; captain, March, 1853; brevet-major, June, 1856; major, May, 1857; brevet-lieut.-colonel, July, 1858; brevet-colonel, September, 1865; colonel commanding, October, 1871. Embarked for Turkey with the 95th Regiment, but remained at Scutari when the Regiment embarked for the Crimea, rejoining in camp before Sebastopol on the 9th Oct. Present at the repulse of the sortie of the 26th October and at Inkerman (severely wounded). Proceeded to India with the Regiment and served throughout the Central India Campaign (despatches). Awarded Crimean medal (2 clasps), Turkish medal, and India medal (1 clasp).	Born 26th Feb. 1824. Commanded 95th, Nov.1871 to June 1875. Died 10th Nov., 1893.
5 Captain the Hon. Eyre Challoner H. Massey (Lord Clarina), R.W.	Appointed ensign 68th Foot, October, 1847; lieutenant, 7th Foot, November, 1851; 31st Foot, July, 1852; captain, January, 1853; captain 95th Foot, June, 1854; brevet-major, November, 1855; major, November, 1857; brevet-lieut.-colonel, July, 1858; brevet-colonel, April, 1865. Joined the 95th in camp before Sebastopol	Born 30th April,1830. Promoted to command of 97th Foot, 1st April, 1873; died 16th Dec., 1897, with

	on the 22nd November, 1854; accompanied the 95th to India and served throughout the Central India Campaign (despatches). Awarded 5th class of the Legion of Honour and of the Medjidie, Crimean medal (1 clasp), Turkish medal, and India medal (1 clasp).	rank of genl., C.B., and Colonel of Durham Light Infantry.
6 Captain the Hon. Edward Sidney Plunkett, L.W.	Appointed ensign, 86th Foot, June, 1836; lieutenant, 95th Foot, June, 1841; captain, March, 1851. Was on half-pay from March, 1851, to July, 1854, when he rejoined the 95th from the Unattached List, arriving in the Crimea 10th Dec., 1854. Accompanied the Regiment to India and served throughout the Central India Campaign (despatches). Awarded 4th class of the Medjidie, Crimean medal (1 clasp), Turkish medal and India medal (1 clasp).	Retired 30th November, 1860. Since deceased.
7 Capt. Henry Foster, L.W.	Appointed ensign 95th Foot, Nov., 1845; lieutenant, June, 1848; captain, September 1854; brevet-major, July, 1858; brevet-lieut.-colonel, March, 1869; major, Oct., 1871. Embarked for Turkey with the 95th, was invalided home, and while at home, was accidentally wounded in the knee by a pistol bullet, and did not arrive in the Crimea till December, 1858. Accompanied the Regiment to India and served throughout the Central India Campaign (despatches). Awarded the India medal (1 clasp).	Died 24th Dec., 1874.
8 Capt. George Lynedoch Carmichael, R.W.	Appointed ensign 95th Regiment, December, 1849; lieutenant, October, 1852; captain, December, 1854; brevet-major, November, 1858. Embarked for Turkey with	Retired 5th April, 1871.

	the 95th and was present at the Alma, at the repulse of the sortie of the 26th October, at Inkerman, and at the fall of Sebastopol. Was Provost Marshal to the army from June, 1855, to the end of the campaign. *Was one of the three officers who served uninterruptedly throughout the campaign without ever being off the strength:* accompanied the 95th to India, and served throughout the Central India Campaign (despatches). Was staff officer to a field column under Major Hon. E. Massey, brigade-major to Rajputana F.F. and also at Neemuch. Awarded 4th class of the Legion of Honour, 5th class Medjidie, Crimean medal (3 clasps), Turkish medal and India medal (1 clasp).	
9 Captain Edmund Davidson Smith, L.W.	Appointed ensign, 95th Foot, April, 1853; lieutenant, June, 1854; captain, June, 1855; embarked for Turkey with the 95th Regiment, and was present at the Alma; was severely wounded in the trenches before Sebastopol on the 17th October, 1854, when he was invalided home. Accompanied the Regiment to India and served throughout the Central India Campaign. Awarded Crimean medal (3 clasps), Turkish medal, and India medal (1 clasp).	Promoted to an unattached Majority, 5th June, 1866. Is now a retired major-general.
10 Capt. Evelyn Bazalgette, R.W.	Appointed ensign, 95th Foot, May, 1853; embarked for Turkey with the Regiment and carried the Regimental Colour at the Alma (twice wounded): rejoined before Sebastopol, as a captain, on the 25th December, 1855. Embarked for India with the 95th.	Killed by the explosion of a magazine near Kotah, Central India, on the 31st Mar., 1857.

	Entitled to Crimean medal (2 clasps), Turkish medal, and India medal (1 clasp).	
11 Captain G. H. Langford-Brooke.	Appointed ensign, 53rd Foot, June, 1853, and exchanged in February, 1854, to the 95th; lieutenant, December, 1854; captain, August, 1856; was on half-pay, November, 1856, to May, 1857. Joined the 95th in Turkey in July, and was present at the Alma (wounded in two places). Proceeded to India with a draft in January, 1858, and served in concluding part of Central India Campaign. Awarded the Crimean medal (1 clasp), Turkish medal, and India medal (1 clasp).	Retired from the service 16th Dec., 1859. Died some years after in Paris, having shot himself accidentally with his revolver
12 Capt. Henry E. Moore, R.W.	Appointed ensign, 35th Foot, September, 1847; lieutenant, May, 1850; captain, November, 1854; when he exchanged to the 95th. Proceeded to India with the Regiment and served in the Central India Campaign. Awarded India medal (1 clasp).	Retired 22nd Jan., 1860.
13 Captain John Wm. Inglis Stockwell, L.W.	Appointed ensign, 95th Foot, August, 1853; lieutenant, December, 1854; captain, May, 1857; major, April, 1873. Joined the 95th in camp before Sebastopol in January, 1855, and served to the end of the siege. Accompanied the 95th to India and served in the Central India Campaign. Awarded 5th class Medjidie, Crimean medal (1 clasp), Turkish medal, and India medal (1 clasp).	Died at Mentone, 29th Mar., 1875.
14 Lieutenant Jonathan Benison, L.W.	Appointed ensign, 95th Foot, June, 1854; lieutenant, December, 1854; captain, November, 1857. Proceeded to the Crimea in December,	Died at Poona on 24th Mar., 1862, aged 26.

	1854, and served until the fall of Sebastopol. Accompanied the Regiment to India and served throughout the Central India Campaign. Awarded the 5th class of the Medjidie, Crimean medal (1 clasp), Turkish medal, and India medal (1 clasp).	
15 Lieut. Charles Frederick Parkinson, R.W.	Appointed ensign, 95th Foot, Sept., 1854; lieutenant, February, 1855; captain, November, 1858; major, December, 1874; lieut.-colonel, July, 1875. Joined the 95th in camp before Sebastopol, February, 1855, and served to the end of the campaign, being wounded in the final assault. Accompanied the 95th to India, and served in the Central India Campaign (despatches). Awarded Crimean medal (1 clasp), Turkish medal, and India medal (1 clasp).	Commanded 95th, 21st July, 1875, to 21st July, 1880. Retired with rank of major-genl.
16 Lieut. John North Crealock, R.W.	Appointed ensign, 95th Foot, October, 1854; lieutenant, February, 1855; captain, May, 1859; brevet-major, July, 1872; major, March, 1875; brevet-lieut.-colonel, November, 1878; lieutenant-colonel commanding, July, 1880; brevet-colonel, November, 1882; major general, January, 1892; Inspector Musketry, Bombay, May, 1860, to May, 1862; A.D.C. to Commander-in-Chief, Bombay, December, 1862, to March, 1864; A.D.C. to C.-in-C., Ireland, August, 1870, to November, 1871; D.A.A.-G. Aldershot, November, 1873, to April, 1874; D.A.Q.-M.-G. Horse Guards, January, 1876, to January, 1878; military secretary, Cape, February, 1878, to July,	Died as Maj.-Genl. Com. Rawul Pindi, Punjab, 25th April, 1895, aged 59.

	1879; A. A.-G., Horse Guards, October, 1879, to September, 1880. Accompanied the 95th Regiment to India and served throughout the Central India Campaign (wounded, despatches). Commanded 2nd Battalion Derbyshire Regiment, August, 1880, to August, 1885, and during the Egyptian Expedition of 1882. Awarded the C.B. India medal (1 clasp), South African medal and clasp, Egyptian medal and Bronze star.	
17 Lieut. George Robertson, R.W.	Appointed ensign, 95th Foot, November, 1854; lieutenant, February, 1855; captain, December, 1859. Joined the 95th before Sebastopol, January, 1855, and served to the end of the campaign. Accompanied the Regiment to India and served in the Central India Campaign. Awarded Crimean medal (1 clasp), 5th class of the Medjidie, Turkish medal, and India medal (1 clasp).	Exchanged to the 25th Foot, May, 1860.
18 Lieut. John Budgen, L.W.	Appointed ensign, 95th Foot, November, 1854; lieutenant, March, 1855; captain, June, 1860. Joined the 95th before Sebastopol in August, 1855, and served to the end of the campaign. Accompanied the Regiment to India and served in the Central India Campaign (despatches). Awarded the Crimean medal (1 clasp), Turkish medal and India medal (1 clasp).	Retired Jan., 1863.
19 Lieut. Robert M. Bonner Maurice, R.W.	Appointed ensign, 95th Foot, in November, 1854; lieutenant, March, 1855; captain, June, 1860. Joined the Regiment before Sebastopol in August, 1855, and	Died of dysentery at Poona, 12th Sept., 1861.

	served to the end of the siege. Accompanied the Regiment to India and served in the Central India Campaign (despatches). Awarded the Crimean medal (1 clasp), Turkish medal, and India medal (1 clasp).	
20 Lieut. John Malone Sexton, R.W.	Was claimed to the 95th from the 75th to serve with an elder brother, and had nearly five years' service as private and non-commissioned officer before promoted ensign in the 95th Regiment, 1854, for Inkerman; lieutenant, March, 1855; adjutant, October, 1855; captain, September, 1861. Accompanied the 95th to the Crimea as colour-sergeant of No. 3 Company, was present at the Alma, the repulse of the Russian sortie of the 26th October, Inkerman, and fall of Sebastopol. Proceeded to India with the 95th and served throughout the Central India Campaign (wounded, despatches). Awarded the 5th class of the Legion of Honour, Crimean medal (3 clasps), Turkish medal and India medal (1 clasp).	Exchanged to the Bengal S.C., 1st Oct., 1870. Retired on Colonel's allowances in 1889 with rank of Major-General.
21 Lieut. Norton Knatchbull, R.W.	Appointed ensign, 95th Foot, December, 1854; lieutenant, March, 1855; captain, November, 1860; major, July, 1875. Joined the 95th before Sebastopol, June, 1855, and served to the end of the siege. Accompanied the Regiment to India and served throughout the Central India Campaign (despatches). Awarded Crimean medal (1 clasp), Turkish medal and India medal (1 clasp).	Retired in 1881 with rank of Col.

22 Lieut. John Joseph Bacon, R.W.	Appointed ensign, 95th Foot, January, 1855; lieutenant, April, 1855; captain, March, 1862. Joined the 95th in the Crimea in July, 1855, and was invalided to Scutari the following month. Embarked for India with the 95th, and served in the Central India Campaign. Awarded Crimean medal (1 clasp), Turkish medal, and India medal (1 clasp).	Retired 30th April, 1866.
23 Lieut. John Henry Waterfall, L.W.	Appointed ensign, 95th, Jan., 1855; lieutenant, June, 1855. Joined the Regiment in camp before Sebastopol in November, 1855, and served to the end of the campaign. Accompanied the Regiment to India in 1857.	Exchanged in July, 1860, to the 5th Light Dragoons; since deceased.
24 Lt. Archbold Macdonnell Rawlins, L.W.	Appointed ensign, 95th Foot, March, 1855; lieutenant, August, 1855; captain, January, 1863; Major, February, 1878. Joined the 95th in camp before Sebastopol towards the end of September, and served to the end of the campaign. Accompanied the Regiment to India and served in the Central India Campaign (despatches). Awarded India medal (1 clasp).	Retired on pension April, 1878; since deceased.
25 Lieut. Henry Gresham Paske, R.W.	Appointed ensign, 95th Foot, in March, 1855; lieutenant, Nov. 1855; adjutant, October, 1861; captain, April, 1866; major, April, 1878. Joined the 95th in camp before Sebastopol, August, 1855, and served to the end of the campaign. Accompanied the Regiment to India and served in the Central India Campaign. Awarded Crimean medal (1 clasp); Turkish medal and India medal (1 clasp).	Retired in 1881 with rank of Col.

26 Lieut. Charles Edward Fisher, R.W.	Appointed ensign, 95th Foot, March, 1855; lieutenant, November, 1855. Joined the 95th in camp before Sebastopol in October, 1855. Accompanied the Regiment to India and served in the Central India Campaign (dangerously wounded). Awarded medal and clasp for Central India.	Transferred to the Bombay S.C., 27th Aug. 1866.
27 Lieut. Joseph Gabbett.	Appointed ensign, 95th Foot, March, 1855; lieutenant, December, 1855; captain, November, 1866. Joined the 95th in the Crimea, October, 1855. Landed in India with a draft in February, 1858, and served in the latter part of Central India Campaign. Awarded India medal and clasp.	Exchanged to the Madras S.C., 28th Oct., 1871. Since deceased.
28 Lt. William R. Willans, R.W.	Appointed ensign, 95th Foot, in April, 1855; lieutenant, February, 1856. Joined the 95th in camp before Sebastopol, January, 1856. Accompanied the Regiment to India and served in the Central India Campaign. Awarded India medal and clasp.	Retired, 28th June, 1861.
29 Ensign Alexander Fawcett, L.W.	Appointed ensign, 95th Foot, May, 1855; lieutenant, February, 1857. Joined the 95th in camp before Sebastopol in January, 1856. Accompanied the Regiment to India and served in the Central India Campaign. Entitled to India medal and clasp.	Killed in action at Beejapore, C.I. 5th Sept., 1858, aged 19.
30 Ensign Charles James Holbrook, L.W.	Appointed ensign, 95th Foot, May, 1855; lieutenant, November, 1857. Joined 95th in camp before Sebastopol, March, 1856. Accompanied the Regiment to India and served in the Central India Campaign. Awarded the India medal and clasp.	Killed by a fall from his horse at Hydrabad, 14th April, 1863, aged 25.

31 Ensign Robert Macnee, L.W.	Appointed ensign, 95th Foot, June, 1855 ; lieutenant, April, 1858. Accompanied the Regiment to India and served in the Central India Campaign. Awarded India medal and clasp.	Died at Karachi, 2nd May, 1866, aged 31.
32 Ensign William Pearson, R.W.	Appointed ensign, 95th Foot, July, 1855 ; lieutenant, November, 1858. Accompanied the Regiment to India and served in the Central India Campaign (despatches). Awarded India medal and clasp.	Exchanged to the 45th Foot, 21st Oct., 1859.
33 Ensign Edward Chapple, L.W.	Appointed ensign, 95th Foot, Aug., 1855 ; lieutenant, May, 1859. Accompanied the Regiment to India and served in the Central India Campaign. Awarded India medal and clasp.	Retired 18th Aug., 1865; since deceased.
34 Ensign Lewis Cubitt, R.W.	Appointed ensign, 95th Foot, Nov., 1855 ; lieutenant, December, 1859. Accompanied the Regiment to India and served in the Central India Campaign. Awarded India medal and clasp.	Exchanged 26th Oct., 1860, to the 26th Foot; since deceased.
35 Ensign Leonard Knipe, L.W.	Appointed ensign, 95th Foot, December, 1855 ; lieutenant, June, 1860. Accompanied the Regiment to India and served in the Central India Campaign. Awarded India medal and clasp.	Exchanged 11th Sept., 1860.
36 Ensign Henry Clement Wilkinson, L.W.	Appointed ensign, 95th Foot, Feb. 1856 ; and accompanied the Regiment to India in 1857; lieutenant, 17th Foot, August, 1859 ; afterwards exchanged to the 16th Lancers and commanded them 1871 to 1877; inspector-general of Auxiliary Cavalry 1877 to 1879; military secretary to C.-in-C. in India, 1880 ; commanded Cavalry Brigade under General	Lieut.-Gen., May, 1894, retired in 1895. Colonel, 4th Dragoon Guards, K.C.B.

	Phayre in the Afghan War; and Indian Cavalry Brigade in Egypt, 1882. Awarded India medal and clasp, the Afghan war medal, C.B. Egyptian medal and clasp, 2nd class of the Medjidie and Khedive's star.	
37 Ensign Andrew McDonald Grote, R.W.	Appointed ensign, 95th Foot, Feb., 1856. Accompanied the Regiment to India and served in the Central India Campaign. Awarded India medal and clasp.	Promoted to lieut. in the 38th Foot, 31st Dec., 1858; since deceased.
38 Ensign Robert Anderson, L.W.	Appointed ensign, 95th Foot, Feb., 1856; lieutenant, November, 1860. Accompanied the Regiment to India and served in the Central India Campaign (despatches). Awarded India medal and clasp.	Exchanged on the 8th July, 1862, to the 37th Foot.
39 Paymaster Maxwell K. Morris, R.W.	Appointed paymaster, 95th Foot, March, 1857; captain, March, 1862. Accompanied the Regiment to India and served in the Central India Campaign. Awarded India medal and clasp.	Exchanged on the 30th Jan., 1869, to the 97th Foot.
40 Quarter-Master John Campbell, R.W.	Had served as a private and non-commissioned officer for nearly 17 years when promoted quarter-master in April, 1854, and had been with the Regiment in Ceylon and Hongkong. Embarked for Turkey with the 95th. *Was one of the three officers who served uninterruptedly throughout the Crimean campaign without ever being off the strength.* Accompanied the 95th to India and served throughout the Central India Campaign. Awarded Crimean medal (3 clasps), Turkish medal and India medal (1 clasp).	Promoted to be paymaster 36th Foot, 22nd Feb., 1868. Retired in 1884, after 47 years' service, and died at Acton, 19th June, 1896, aged 72, having enlisted at the age of 14.

41 Surgeon John Ewing, R.W.	Appointed assistant surgeon, May, 1841; surgeon, March, 1852. Was attached to the 95th in the Crimea from September, 1855, to June, 1856. Accompanied the 95th to India and served in the Central India Campaign. Awarded India medal and clasp.	Exchanged to the Staff 23rd May, 1859.
42 Assistant-Surgeon Robert Ferguson, L.W.	Appointed to the 95th Regiment, April, 1853. Embarked for Turkey with the Regiment and was present at the Alma, the sortie of the 26th October, Inkerman, and fall of Sebastopol. *Was one of the three officers who served uninterruptedly throughout the campaign without ever being off the strength.* Accompanied the Regiment to India. Crimean medal (3 clasps) and Turkish medal.	Died at Deesa on the 26th January, 1858.
43 Assistant-Surgeon John Clarke, R.W.	Appointed to the 95th Regiment, March, 1854. Embarked for Turkey with the Regiment and was present at the Alma, the repulse of the sortie of the 26th October, Inkerman, and fall of Sebastopol. Accompanied the Regiment to India and served in the Central India Campaign (despatches). Awarded Crimean medal (3 clasps), Turkish medal, and India medal (1 clasp).	Died of yellow fever in the West Indies, having left the 95th in Dec., 1860.
44 Assistant-Surgeon William Sharpe.	Appointed to the 95th, March, 1858. Joined in August of that year, and served in latter part of Central India Campaign. Awarded India medal and clasp.	Exchanged to the Staff in July, 1860.

APPENDIX. 81

Names of the Sergeants who took part in the Campaign.

Sgt.-Maj.	William Ashfield	Sergeant	Thomas Death
Q.M.S.	Adam Lambert	,,	William Draycott
P.M.S.	John Hogan	,,	Thomas Farr
Arm. S.	John Carpenter	,,	George Finney
Dr. Major	Charles McDowell	,,	John Goldsmith
Hosp. S.	Charles Bramley	,,	William Guy
O.R.S.	William Reid	,,	Edwin Halling
Cr.-Sgt.	Jonas Woolnough	,,	William Hutson
,,	John Brick	,,	William Kearin
,,	James Crangle	,,	Patrick McKernon
,,	John Gooding	,,	Denis Mahoney
,,	William Turner	,,	Alfred Merriman
,,	George Garrett	,,	Charles W. Murphy
,,	Robert Hamilton	,,	William Nelson
,,	James O'Donnell	,,	Robert Potts
Sergeant	William Ahern	,,	Robert Richardson
,,	John Bowen	,,	Henry Seal
,,	Patrick Brick	,,	— Sullivan
,,	Henry Cook	,,	Edward Reynolds
,,	Charles Cooper	,,	Samuel Hunter

G

APPENDIX B.

Names of Officers, Non-commissioned Officers, and men, killed, wounded, and died in the Central India Campaign.

KILLED.

Rank.	Name.	Place.	Date.	Nature of Casualty.
Captain	E. Bazalgette	Kotah	31st March, 1857	
Lieutenant	A. Fawcett	Beejapore	5th Sept., 1858	
Private	George Green	Kotah	30th March, 1858	
,,	Joseph Shaw	Gwalior	19th June, 1858	

WOUNDED.

Rank.	Name.	Place.	Date.	Nature of Casualty.
Lieut.-Colonel	J. A. R. Raines	Gwalior	19th June, 1858	Severely, left arm
Lieutenant	J. N. Crealock	Kotah-ki-Serai	17th June, 1858	Severely
,,	J. M. Sexton	Gwalior	19th June, 1858	Burnt, explosion
,,	C. E. Fisher	Powree	21st Aug., 1858	Dangerously, chest
Corporal	Joseph Hunt	Gwalior	19th June, 1858	Burnt, explosion
Private	John Bird	Kotah-ki-Serai	17th June, 1858	Severely
,,	William Brooks	Koondrye	14th Nov., 1858	Severely

APPENDIX. 83

WOUNDED—*continued.*

Rank.	Name.	Place.	Date.	Nature of Casualty.
Private	Henry Cole	Kotah-ki-Serai	17th June, 1858	Severely. Died at Seepree, 21 Oct., 1858
,,	Robert Dutton	Kotah-ki-Serai	17th June, 1858	Severely
,,	Olven Grady	Rowa...	6th Jan, 1858	Dangerously
,,	William Hall	Kotah-ki-Serai	17th June, 1858	Mortally
,,	George Hennon	Rowa...	6th Jan, 1858	
,,	Michael Hogan	Gwalior	19th June, 1858	Severely contused
,,	Thos. Johnson	Gwalior	18th June, 1858	Severely contused
,,	Jos. McCartney	Gwalior	19th June, 1858	Severely contused
,,	John McHale	Powree	21st Aug., 1858	Severely wounded
,,	Bernard McQuirt	Rowa...	6th Jan, 1858	Dangerously
,,	Hugh Nelson	Gwalior	19th June, 1858	Dangerously
,,	John O'Keefe	Beejapore	5th Sept., 1858	Dangerously: Died
,,	Patrick O'Neill	Kotah	28th March, 1858	Mortally
,,	Charles Parsons	Beejapore	5th Sept., 1858	Severely
,,	William Pike	Gwalior	19th June, 1858	Severely
,,	Henry Robinson	Gwalior	18th June, 1858	Slightly
,,	Edward Rodden	Gwalior	19th June, 1858	Slightly
,,	James Suttle	Kotah-ki-Serai	17th June, 1858	Severely contused
,,	Thos. Williams	Beejapore	5th Sept., 1858	Dangerously
,,	James Swan	Kotah-ki-Serai	17th June, 1858	Slightly

Names of those who died during the Campaign.

Rank.	Name.	Date.	
Ast. Surg.	Robert Fergusson	26th Jan., 1858	Deesa.
Sergeant	Charles Cooper	9th May, 1858	
Corporal	William Gourley	15th Dec., 1858	CampBurode
,,	Charles Philp	23rd May, 1858	
Drummer	John Thos. Bailey	19th June, 1858	
,,	Patrick Gorman	9th May, 1858	
Private	Geo. Ashbrook	26th May, 1858	
,,	Benjamin Bailey	5th July, 1858	
,,	Peter Brogan	3rd June, 1858	
,,	Samuel Clements	5th Feb., 1858	Awah.
,,	John Cole	30th Sept., 1858	
,,	Michael Colonans	22nd May, 1858	
,,	Joseph Cooper	12th June, 1858	
,,	Bernard Corry	20th June, 1858	
,,	William Desmond	7th May, 1858	
,,	John Douglass	11th May, 1858	
,,	Thomas Finn	24th June, 1858	
,,	George Gardiner	13th June, 1859	CampBurode
,,	John Gimson	11th June, 1858	
,,	John Hambleton	23rd June, 1858	
,,	Robert Hodge	12th June, 1858	
,,	William Jones	10th May, 1858	
,,	Matthew McGarry	26th May, 1858	
,,	Thomas Murray	3rd Nov., 1858	Camp Tall.
,,	John Nash	14th June, 1858	
,,	Henry Parker	31st Aug., 1858	
,,	Charles Pitcher	16th Nov., 1858	Seepree.
,,	Joseph Pollard	10th June, 1858	
,,	James Scott	15th Aug., 1858	
,,	John Shaw	1st Nov., 1858	
,,	Joseph Sodon	11th June, 1858	
,,	Edward Spoor	26th Mar., 1858	Kotah.
,,	John Stevenson	10th Jan., 1859	Drowned, Camp Etawah.
,,	John Ward	19th Aug., 1858	
,,	John Thos. Watson	17th June, 1858	
,,	William Yeomans	6th Jan., 1859	Camp Narghar.

APPENDIX C.

Itinerary of the march of the Headquarter Wing, 95th Regiment, through Cutch, Rajputana, and Central India, from January, 1858, to May, 1859.

Date.		Camp.	Miles.	
1858.				
Jan.	1	Tankaria		
,,	2	Jumbooseer	11	
,,	3	Goasud	10	
,,	4	Padra	9	
,,	5	Baroda	12	Halt.
,,	7	Wassud	10	
,,	8	Annundmagri	9	
,,	9	Neriad	7	
,,	10	Kaira	10	Halt.
,,	12	Lallee	10	
,,	13	Ahmedabad	12	Halt.
,,	19	Moved Camp	3	Crossed river.
,,	20	Adaulij	9	
,,	21	Panshur	13	
,,	22	Langnay	10	
,,	23	Mysana	14	Halt.
,,	25	Oonja	12	
,,	26	Sidpur	11	
,,	27	Mayta	16	
,,	28	Gud	11	
,,	29	Deesa	18	Halt.
Feb.	2	Donpoora	12	
,,	3	Pantawara	13	
,,	4	Muddar	12	
,,	5	Reodar	11	
,,	6	Anadra	12	Halt.
,,	8	Meera		
,,	9	Seerohee	11	

CENTRAL INDIAN CAMPAIGN.

Date.		Camp.	Miles.	
Feb.	10	Palree	14	Halt.
,,	13	Erinpoora	16	
,,	14	Sanderaó	10	
,,	15	Dhola-ka-gaun	10	
,,	16	Goondoze	12	
,,	17	Pallee	10	Halt.
,,	19	Jadun	11	
,,	20	Soojit	10	
,,	21	Chundrawul	9	
,,	22	Joota	12	
,,	23	Burr	11	
,,	24	Nyanuggur	10	Halt.
,,	26	Khurwar	11	
,,	27	Nusseerabad	18	Halt.
March	10	Surana	13	
,,	11	Surwar	$11\frac{1}{4}$	
,,	12	Kekree	$11\frac{1}{2}$	
,,	13	Para	7	Halt.
,,	15	Sawar	9	
,,	16	Jhajpoor	$10\frac{1}{2}$	
,,	17	Etrudah	10	
,,	18	Nowgaum	$12\frac{1}{2}$	
,,	19	Boondee	14	Halt.
,,	21	Talra	18	
,,	22	Kotah	14	Halt.
April	19	Jugpoora	10	
,,	20	Hunotea	8	
,,	21	Ahmedpoora	5	
,,	22	Bahwara	$9\frac{1}{2}$	
,,	23	Mukundura	9	
,,	24	Khyrabad	$11\frac{1}{2}$	Bivouac.
,,	25	Juhapatun	14	
,,	26	Usnaweer	10	Halt.
,,	28	Bunniagaum	14	
,,	29	Sartnul	10	
,,	30	Barode	12	
May	1	Chuprah	12	Halt.
,,	5	Shikarpoor	6	
,,	6	Nargheer	14	
,,	7	Paidon	9	Bivouac.
,,	9	Futtehghur	10	
,,	10	Purwahi	9	
,,	11	Jeyghur	5	

APPENDIX.

Date.		Camp.	Miles.	
May	12	Goona	12	Halt.
,,	19		2	Moved camp.
,,	21	Pinneguthi	12	
,,	22	Shadowra	7½	
,,	23	Pucka	10	
,,	24	Pharee	4	
,,	25	Khowarson	3	
,,	26	Chundaree	4	Halt.
June	1	Mahouli	10	
,,	2	Esaghar	13	
,,	3	Kasaun	12	
,,	4	Paihouli	5½	
,,	5	Kolarose	7	
,,	6	Seepree	14	Halt.
,,	10	Suttonwaree	11	
,,	11	Chorkayra	11½	
,,	12	Mahouli	12	
,,	13	Arone	10	
,,	14	Bunwar	10	Halt.
,,	16	Antree	9	
,,	17	Kotah-ki-Serai	9	
,,	18	Gwalior	5	Halt.
July	21	Punniar	9	
,,	22	Mahona	19	Halt.
,,	25	Chorkayra	11	Halt.
,,	27	Suttonwaree	13	
,,	28	Seepree	11	Halt.
Aug.	5	Jeree	14	
,,	6	Powree	6	Halt.
,,	23	Pursuit of enemy	24	Halt.
,,	25	Powree	24	Halt.
,,	30	Jeree	6	
,,	31	Seepree	14	
Sept.	3	Sissay	7	Halt.
,,	16	Laknasa	12	Halt.
,,	19	Badoona	13	
,,	20	Meana	13	
,,	21	Goona	18	Halt.
,,	25	Badhoor	14	Halt.
,,	28	Ammoda	4	Halt.
,,	30	Burkaria	6	
Oct.	1	Goona	12	
,,	2	Poona-Kaira	12	

CENTRAL INDIAN CAMPAIGN.

Date.		Camp.	Miles.	
Oct.	3	Nayaserai	12	
,,	4	Banshoor	14	
,,	5	Esaghar	13	Halt.
,,	10	Mahouli	15	
,,	11	Mowrowe	8	
,,	12	Serai	7	Halt.
,,	14	Katighaut	16	
,,	15	Serai	16	
,,	16	Morane	12	
,,	17	Ramnugger	3	
,,	18	Jalapoor	3	Halt.
,,	23	Serai	18	
,,	24	Mongrowlee	14	
,,	25	Buronsee	10	Halt.
,,	30	Mullaghar	12	Halt.
Nov.	1	Moondiah	11	
,,	2	Tall	13	Halt.
,,	4	Seronge	14	
,,	5	Deepnakhyra...	12	Halt.
,,	8	Bahadurpoor	11	Halt.
,,	10	Godowlie	12	Halt.
,,	12	Burkaria	16	
,,	13	Rajpoor	12	Bivouac.
,,	16	Attkaria	8	
,,	17	Tomassa	14	
,,	18	Mungrowlee	8	Halt.
,,	22	Oondanah	13	
,,	23	Deepnakhyra...	10	Halt.
,,	26	Seronge	12	Halt.
Dec.	1	Moondiah	17	
,,	2	Muksudenghur	15	
,,	3	Sutnia...	10	
,,	4	Browna	16	Halt.
,,	12	Sutnia...	16	
,,	13	Barode	10	
,,	14	Lutheree	10	
,,	15	Roosie	12	
,,	16	Seronge	10	
,,	21	Kolapoor	22	
,,	22	Kutchnakyra...	6	
,,	23	Seronge	16	Halt.
,,	27	Kutchnakyra...	16	
,,	28	Mootee	8	

APPENDIX.

Date.		Camp.	Miles.	
Dec.	29	Bursud	18	
,,	31	Bomahud		
1859.				
Jan.	1	Chupra	26	
,,	2	Kaira	9	
,,	3	Futtehghur	9	Halt.
,,	5	Narghar	10	
,,	6	Kailwarra	16	
,,	7	Relawan	14	
,,	8	Mungrowlee	11	
,,	9	Etawah	17	
,,	10	Turiah...	10	
,,	11	Indraghar	10	
,,	12	Katowlee	13	Halt.
,,	14	Rampoorah	6	
,,	15	Coonairah	6	Halt.
,,	17	Nuggar	10	
,,	18	Dorian	10	
,,	21	Lambah	10	
,,	22	Tonk	9	Halt
,,	28	Moved camp	3	
Feb.	5	Moved camp	3	
,,	18	Boongariah	16	
,,	19	Boolgarah	24	
,,	20	Dooblana	12	
,,	21	Boondee	13	
,,	22	Baji Dagroo	14	
,,	23	Kotah	14	Halt.
,,	25	Keytoni	$9\frac{1}{2}$	
,,	26	Kugooree	$11\frac{1}{2}$	
,,	27	Sangrode	15	
,,	28	Bhawulpoora...	$9\frac{1}{2}$	
March	1	Luckerpoora	9	
,,	2	Koondee	$12\frac{1}{4}$	
,,	3	Chupra	$12\frac{1}{2}$	Halt.
,,	6	Banagong	18	
,,	7	Oonah	11	
,,	8	Bursad	9	
,,	24	Raghoghar	13	Halt.
,,	29	Bursad	14	
,,	30	Muksudenghar	18	Halt.
April	2	Goonarah	14	Halt.
,,	5	Muksudenghar	14	Halt.

CENTRAL INDIAN CAMPAIGN.

Date.	Camp.	Miles.	
April 13	Jumeneer	10	Halt.
,, 25	Bursad	8	
,, 26	Chanchora	13	
,, 27	Munhoor Thana	15	
,, 28	Chorella	14	
,, 29	Bunniaghat	14	
,, 30	Uniwar	14	
May 1	Jalapatten	14	Halt.
,, 3	Rajpoor	12	
,, 4	Oosara-Moolghar	14	
,, 5	Bahmpoor	8	Halt.
,, 7	Bumowrie	15	
,, 8	Rampoora	10	Halt.
,, 10	Kikri-sirr	12	
,, 11	Sawun	12	
,, 12	Neemuch	12	

Total length of march, 2492 miles.

www.ingramcontent.com/pod-product-compliance
Lightning Source LLC
Chambersburg PA
CBHW032129090426
42743CB00007B/532